"Isak Dinesen"
and Karen Blixen

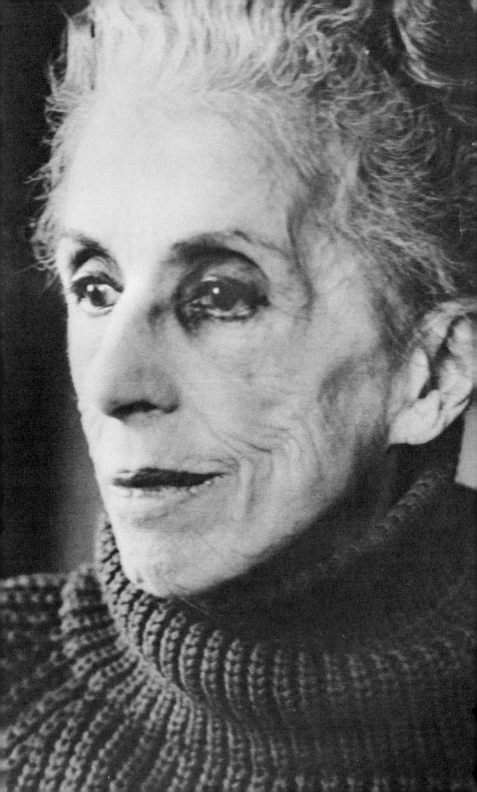

"ISAK DINESEN"
and
KAREN BLIXEN

The Mask
and The Reality

DONALD HANNAH

Senior Lecturer in English
at the University of Aarhus, Denmark

RANDOM HOUSE
New York

TO INGE

CONTENTS

5

35764

ACKNOWLEDGEMENTS

I have much pleasure in acknowledging the kind assistance I have received, while working on this book, from various individuals and institutions.

I am particularly indebted to The Rungstedlund Foundation for granting me permission to consult Isak Dinesen's papers and MSS, and for allowing me to publish *The Revenge of Truth* as an appendix to this book. I also wish to thank Miss Clara Svendsen for discussing points with me in connection with this material and for providing some valuable suggestions included in this study. Mr Thomas Dinesen, V.C., kindly discussed several aspects of his sister's life and work, and I am very grateful for this.

I wish to place on record two further debts. The late Professor Rosemond Tuve was the person who first suggested some years ago that I should start work on Isak Dinesen. I am, in addition, indebted to the late Greta Hort, formerly Professor of English Literature, University of Aarhus, for the interest she showed in the initial stages of this study.

I have also greatly profited from encouragement and advice from the following: Miss Anna Rutherford, lecturer in English and Commonwealth Literature, University of Aarhus; Professor J. C. Reid, University of Auckland; Professor G. R. Hibbard, University of Waterloo, Ontario; Mr B. Jacobsen, lecturer, School of Commerce, Aarhus, and Mr J. Huntington, director, Putnam & Co. Ltd. I am deeply appreciative of the generosity with which they all offered much time and trouble to assist me.

The Rask-Ørsted Foundation, Denmark, awarded me a grant for financial assistance with this project, and I wish to express my thanks for their support.

Part of chapter IV was first published in *The Sewanee Review*, Vol. LXXI, No. 4, 1963, copyright by The University of the South, and I am grateful to the editor for permission to include extracts from this article.

ACKNOWLEDGEMENTS

My thanks must also be extended to the secretarial staff of the English department, University of Aarhus, for all the trouble they have had to decipher my MS, and to Mrs J. Carlsen for the patient care with which she typed an earlier draft.

To all these, and to others who have helped me in various ways, I express my very sincere appreciation and grateful thanks.

DONALD HANNAH

PART I

THE DIFFERENT LIVES OF KAREN BLIXEN

I

The Early Phase:
Karen Dinesen

Baroness Karen Blixen-Finecke combined several quite different figures in one and the same person and during the various stages of her life it would have been impossible for even the closest observer to predict what the next would bring forth. There was Karen Dinesen, the school-girl, who filled her school-books with routine compositions and exercises and with highly imaginative childish stories and poems as well. Then, as a young woman in the first decade of the twentieth century, she took part in the life of the fashionable world of upper-class Copenhagen with its round of parties, balls and receptions, but, side by side with this, she went on writing, and showed so much promise that three of her stories were published in Danish periodicals, all of them, however, under a pseudonym. Moreover there was nothing whatever in the subject-matter of these short stories by 'Osceola' to lead the reader to identify the author as the young Karen Dinesen, apparently intent only upon when the next ball of the season would be held.

The next stage was embarked upon when she left all this behind her at the end of 1913 and started an utterly different life by marrying a Swedish cousin, Baron Bror von Blixen-Finecke, and joining the early white settlers in the newly-established British colony in East Africa. They took a farm not far from Nairobi, and Karen Blixen devoted over seventeen years of her life to all the various activities which running a farm of six thousand acres in a new country entailed. She loved her life there so deeply, with its mixture of joy, hardship and even suffering (all so movingly recorded in *Out of Africa*) that her only wish was to spend the rest of her days as a farmer in Kenya.

When, however, the farm ran into so much debt that it was impossible to go on, she returned to Denmark, dedicated herself henceforth to the vocation of a writer, and established an international reputation as the author Isak Dinesen. Thus 'Isak Dinesen', the pseudonymous author of four collections of stories, known at first solely by the name on the covers of their books, is the same person who categorically stated at the age of twenty that she had no intention of ever becoming what she described as 'a piece of printed matter'.

Karen Blixen and 'Isak Dinesen': as Karen Blixen, the author of *Out of Africa*, a book which graphically recounts her experience in Kenya and brings home to the reader the nature of her daily life there; as 'Isak Dinesen', the writer of tales, each of them finely-wrought and highly imaginative, many of them set at least a century ago, and all of them utterly remote from ordinary daily life. What is the explanation of this difference? In what ways are her stories like *Out of Africa*? What attitudes and beliefs do they display in common? Or, to frame the question in another way: in what sense are Isak Dinesen and Karen Blixen really one and the same person?

Although Isak Dinesen's stories are never directly autobiographical, a very close connection can still be traced between her life and her work. While this is true for many other writers, with Isak Dinesen the part her life played in determining the nature of her art is so unusual that it becomes one of the distinguishing features of her work. One must therefore preface a discussion of it by considering her life in more detail; only then can a clearer insight be gained into both the work and the personality of this enigmatic writer.

Karen Dinesen was born in 1885 at Rungstedlund near the small town of Rungsted which lies on the coast about fifteen miles to the north of Copenhagen. The small estate with some adjoining land had been bought by her father six years previously. Today only a small wooded park of some forty acres remains of the original estate, and the surrounding countryside of north Zealand—in some ways rather reminiscent of parts of Surrey—has also greatly changed. Lying so near Copenhagen it is a favourite residential area, and Rungsted itself, which Isak Dinesen knew in her early days as a small fishing village surrounded by farm-land, is now really an outer suburb. Rungstedlund is an old and charming-looking house, but not a particularly imposing one. For some centuries it was used as an inn, it has been added to and changed again over many years, and at the end of the eighteeenth century it acquired associations with Danish literature when the poet, Johannes Ewald, stayed for some time at the inn and wrote 'Rungsteds Lyksaligheder' (The Delights of Rungsted) there. The house, with the park lying behind it, is set only a few yards back from the busy coast road between Copenhagen and Elsinore, and has a fine view of the coast of Sweden and of the narrow straits leading into the Baltic. It was here that Karen Dinesen was brought up; it was to this home that she returned after her years in Kenya, and it was here, among these surroundings, that she lived for the rest of her life.

Her father, Wilhelm Dinesen, was a colourful and adventurous figure who fought in several wars in Europe including the Prusso-Danish conflict of 1864, and who lived for two years among Indian tribes in the United States. The memory of her father and his unusual life seems to have exerted a strong influence on Isak Dinesen: throughout her life she maintained that she took after him, and this was obviously a source of considerable pride. She based one of her most romantic characters, Ib Angel in 'Copenhagen Season', upon him, and in 1958, more than sixty years after his death, she gave a talk on the Danish radio which revealed her admiration for him. She described how, as a seventeen-year-old lieutenant he had taken part in the Prusso-Danish war, and went on:

> . . . later, as a French officer, he went through the Franco-Prussian war. During the Paris Commune he saw the barricades being built and French blood being shed in French streets. He turned away from Europe and its civilisation and lived for three years among Indians in North America without seeing another white man. He was a skilful and successful trapper, but he spent the money he earned on his Indian friends. The Indians called him 'Boganis'. Here at Rungstedlund, under that name, he wrote his *Jagtbreve*—a

hunter's diary, full of the love of nature, of the seasons, animals and birds.[1]

This is, naturally enough, a partial portrait—it omits, for example, that another reason for leaving Europe was the unhappy love-affair which is also treated in 'Copenhagen Season'— but that it is also one not far from the whole truth is corroborated by Georg Brandes, the distinguished Danish writer and critic. In an essay on Wilhelm Dinesen published in 1889 he remarked that 'he loves war for its own sake with the love of a soldier and of an artist. He thinks (even in *Jagtbreve*) that nothing embellishes a landscape more than soldiers fighting', and he goes on to sum up his character in one sentence: 'He looked what he really was—a dreamer in broad daylight.'[2] Wilhelm Dinesen seems, in fact, to have been a highly gifted man, with a restless temperament, unable to reconcile himself to a settled way of life or to devote his talents to any very specific aim. As well as running his estate and writing his hunting letters he took part in discussions of various social and political questions and wrote about them. In 1892 he followed these interests up by becoming a member of the Danish parliament, staying in lodgings in Copenhagen while it was in session; and it was there in 1895, when Karen Dinesen was ten years old, that he hanged himself. The reason for his suicide was never fully established, but according to *The Life and Destiny of Isak Dinesen* she herself in later years believed that her father's anxiety over an incurable illness that would make him a burden upon his family was his motive.[3] His wife was left to bring up the five children alone.

Mrs Dinesen was clearly a woman with a mind and a personality of her own; equally clearly it was one very different from her late husband's—and from her daughter's. Her own mother lived at Folehave, near Rungstedlund, together with an unmarried daughter, Bess Westenholz. This maiden aunt was a redoubtable character; a pioneer of women's rights and female

[1] The talk is published in *Hilsen til Otto Gelsted*, Århus, 1958, pp. 28–29.

[2] *Samlede Skrifter*, Vol. III, Copenhagen, 1919, pp. 189 and 196.

[3] op. cit. edited by Clara Svendsen and Frans Lasson, New York, 1970. p. 40.

emancipation, she was also a pillar of the Unitarian Church in Denmark. She and Karen Dinesen often clashed in a conflict of wills, and many years later her rebellious niece confided to her biographer, Parmenia Migel, that 'one of my main reasons for going to Africa later was to escape from the tyranny of this aunt'.[1] Although there is probably a considerable amount of exaggeration in this remark, there is still a modicum of truth which sufficiently illustrates their relationship. In any case, Folehave became the children's second home, Karen Dinesen's grandmother and aunt exerted a strict Victorian influence on the Dinesen household and closely watched over the children's upbringing. It was in this environment that Karen Dinesen passed her childhood, not even leaving home to go to school, but instead receiving lessons, superintended by Mrs Dinesen and by her grandmother, from a retired school-teacher living in Rungsted. In later life Isak Dinesen made no secret of the fact that she had often been unhappy in the confines of this circle. '"I was like my father's family,"' she told Robert Langbaum, for example, '"My grandmother did not understand me. She liked my sisters better. I was very unhappy as a child."'[2]

Occasionally, during the summer holidays, the Dinesens stayed with their father's brother, who lived on a large estate called Katholm, in Jutland, where her father had been brought up with his brother and sisters. It was through her visits there and to other manors and castles that Karen Dinesen saw the life of the aristocracy from the inside, for, although the Dinesens did not strictly belong to the ranks of the Danish nobility by birth, nevertheless they did have various connections with it through marriage. It is clear that she felt strongly drawn to this way of life and its beliefs, above all, to its sense of *noblesse oblige*. As a writer she made this sense of aristocratic duty and responsibility a major theme in one of her greatest stories, 'Sorrow-Acre', and this same principle formed the corner-stone of her relations with the Africans living on her farm in Kenya. As a child, however, these visits to Katholm, and the accounts

[1] Parmenia Migel: *Titania. The Biography of Isak Dinesen*, New York, 1967, p. 16.

[2] Robert Langbaum: *The Gayety of Vision. A Study of Isak Dinesen's Art*, New York, 1965, p. 39.

she heard of the kind of life her father had spent there as a youth, only served to underline the contrast this made with her own life at Rungstedlund.

What was the nature of this contrast and what did her father's family represent for her? The answer is best given in Isak Dinesen's own words from 'Copenhagen Season', where the life of the 'Angel' family at Ballegaard (the name given to Katholm) in her father's time, is described in the following glowing terms:

> Two or three strong and strange characteristics ran through the nature of the whole brood.
>
> One of these was a great, wild happiness at being alive, what in French is called *la joie de vivre*. Each single thing included in daily human existence—drawing breath, waking up or falling asleep, running, dancing and whistling, food and wine, animals and the four elements themselves—called forth in them a rapture like that of a very young animal, the ecstacy of a foal let loose in a paddock. They would count a flight of geese against the sun, the hours to a coming ball or their last coins of money at the gambling table with the same intense fervour, and lose themselves in a friend's sad love-story or in the putting together of a fishing-rod with the energy of a person throwing himself into the sea. They were natural connoisseurs of wine and food, but munched with equal delight the dry black bread carried about in their pockets for feeding their horses. They were quiet in their manners and least of all self-centred, but they radiated a turbulent content, and their pride in being alive was almost vainglorious.[1]

To the young girl, her father's youth with all its ardour and freedom must have seemed an utterly different world from the one she herself was living in, and the contrast between a bourgeois attitude of cautious prudence and respectability and an aristocratic disdain of convention is one which much later was to appear in several of her tales. She had already begun writing small stories even before his death (according to Miss Clara Svendsen, her secretary for many years, she began writing about the age of eight), and it is not surprising to find her turning increasingly to this activity. Immersed in it, she could escape from some of the surrounding realities. The impetus behind

[1] *Last Tales*, New York, 1957, pp. 260–261.

this writing and the urge she felt to tell stories aloud were compelling ones. On a record of extracts from two of her stories she made in Denmark towards the end of her life, she remembered how, as a child, she would often start telling one of her sisters a story just as they were getting ready to go to bed. '"She would be in despair. 'Can't you stop, just for tonight?' she would say. 'Can't I be left in peace, just tonight?' 'No, I can't,' I would say, 'it isn't possible. We must go on.'"'

If this persistence has its slightly ludicrous side even to Isak Dinesen herself, it still marks the emergence of a characteristic trait. By resorting to telling stories and thus giving free play to her fantasy, she established a pattern of behaviour in these early years to which she was to return as an adult. As a child, she turned from life to art—an art full of wild childish fantasy and romance; there she could find freedom for the imagination to range, one from which she was barred in life. To say this is to place the blame—if indeed there is any—neither on the home nor on the child. Given a vivid imagination, a talent for making up stories, together with a spirited temperament chafing at the bonds imposed by a strict childhood, such a reaction is almost bound to follow. And in reacting in this way she was only doing something which many other writers had done before her; Karen Dinesen created no such complex and self-contained fantasy world like the Brontës' Angria or Gondal, but she did write many stories, poems and short plays. In some of this activity her brothers and sisters also joined; one of these plays (revised and published much later, in 1926, as *Sandhedens Hævn* [*The Revenge of Truth*]) was first written to be performed by the children at Rungstedlund. Several of these stories can be found amongst her papers and manuscripts. Brandes had described Wilhelm Dinesen as a dreamer in broad daylight; so too was his daughter, and these stories constitute tangible evidence of this.

In the introduction written by her brother, Thomas Dinesen, to a collection of memorial essays published after her death there is a passage in which he recalls the evenings in summer when the family used to sit on the verandah at Rungstedlund, and he heard his sister either reciting verse she had written or talking of her aims in life. He remembered one evening in particular when she spoke of how she had once been carried away by enthusiasm for the great historical figures who took part in the French Revolution. '"How," she had wondered, "could a girl living in this deadly boring twentieth century . . . gain access to that heroic world?"' Perhaps by going hungry, she had thought. And she described how, although she had to eat something whilst at home, whenever she went into town, she left the packed lunch under the seat in the railway compartment.[1]

From someone who was, according to Mr Dinesen, at least twenty at the time, the form which her protest took against life 'in this deadly boring twentieth century' may strike us as decidedly odd. (It also seemed so to Thomas Dinesen at the time, although he writes that later in life he was not so sure.) Nevertheless, the discontent and frustration she felt at this time also points to what was the main factor dictating her choice of subject-matter in the stories dating even from her early adult life. One of these, called 'Grjotgard Ålvesøn og Aud' was written about the same time as she made these remarks. It was written in Danish, left unfinished, and only published posthumously.[2] The story is based on one of the Norse sagas that Mrs Dinesen used to read aloud to the children in the evenings, and in the foreword to the collection of Isak Dinesen's early tales, Thomas Dinesen says that 'we children had identified ourselves with the attitudes and the ideas of those times'.[3]

Two other stories were published in 1907 and a third in 1909. In one of them, 'Eneboerne' (The Hermits), a married couple live in solitude on an island far from any contact with civilisation; the husband devotes himself to his studies whilst the wife, left alone, is visited by a ghost, who eventually entices her away with him so that she dies. In the other, 'Pløjeren' (The Ploughman) a witch has passed the curse of her blood on to her son. The spell of the supernatural is finally broken when

---

[1] *Karen Blixen*, edited by Clara Svendsen and Ole Wivel, Copenhagen, 1962, pp. 11–12.
[2] Included in the collection of early stories, *Osceola*, Copenhagen, 1962.
[3] *Osceola*, p. 9.

he is brought into communion with nature by the heroine, who sets him to plough the fields. The last story published at this time, 'Familien de Cats' (The de Cats Family), does not have the same highly romantic quality, but it is made equally remote from the present by being set in Amsterdam at the end of the eighteenth century. Although these stories were quite favourably received, Karen Dinesen had no ambitions at that time to make a career for herself as a writer; it was at this stage that she remarked that she did not want to become a piece of printed matter. 'I published a few short stories in literary reviews in Denmark, when I was twenty years old,' she told Eugene Walter in an interview published in the *Paris Review*, 'and the reviews encouraged me but I didn't go on—I don't know, I think I had an intuitive fear of being trapped.'[1]

Her first real chance to break away in some degree from home came when she started to attend a school of design in Copenhagen; later she enrolled as a student at the Danish Royal Academy of Art. In 1910 she spent some time in Paris, ostensibly with the intention of studying art further, but, in reality, seeing as much of the life of Paris as possible. The period she spent at the Royal Academy was to bear fruit in later years when she based a character, Professor Sivertsen, in 'Copenhagen Season', on one of her teachers there, and she also used the same person as the model for a character in an unpublished story called 'Carnival'. But the actual training she received as an art student was also not without its effect upon her. In a newspaper interview in 1950, which gives much valuable information about her view of art, she said that she could still not decide whether she loved poetry, music or the visual arts best.[2] Her papers and manuscripts,[3] abounding with small sketches doodled in the margins or with more ambitious full-page ones, testify to the interest in the visual arts maintained throughout her life, and some of her paintings are still hanging in the rooms at Rungstedlund—three of these are reproduced in *Shadows on the Grass*. However, although her work shows considerable

[1] op. cit. No. 14, Autumn, 1956, pp. 51–52.
[2] *Berlingske Aftenavis*, 24th June, 1950.
[3] All references to Isak Dinesen's Manuscripts are to those now kept in the Royal Library, Copenhagen.

talent, the chief point for us lies in what her interest in art and its study meant for her as a writer. And it is worth considering this in a little more detail.

In the interview she mentions some specific paintings which were sources of direct inspiration for some of her stories. Courbet's painting of two young Englishwomen on a balcony, for example, gave her the main theme for 'The Invincible Slave-Owners', and she also mentions a painting which immediately suggested the idea for 'A Consolatory Tale'—she could not actually remember which painting it was. It seems probable that she could also have furnished other examples, but even so, it is doubtful how much light they would have thrown on the individual tale, for this last remark about 'A Consolatory Tale' gives a clue to the way in which her creative faculties operated in this respect. With that story the initial stimulus had become absorbed into the total process of composition so that the particular painting giving rise to the story had been forgotten. And one may suspect a similar process took place with other stories.

Isak Dinesen's life-long interest in painting is also reflected by the way in which her imagination in the tales frequently operates in visual terms. She writes like a painter. The striking description of the countryside in the opening paragraphs of 'Sorrow-Acre' is but one example of this:

The low, undulating Danish landscape was silent and serene, mysteriously wide-awake, in the hour before sunrise. There was not a cloud in the pale sky, not a shadow along the dim, pearly fields, hills and woods . . . The irregular mosaic of meadows and cornlands was a picture, in timid green and yellow of the people's struggle for its daily bread . . . On a distant hill the immovable wings of a windmill, in a small blue cross against the sky, de-lineated a later stage in the career of the bread. The blurred out-line of thatched roofs,—a low, brown growth of the earth,—where the huts of the village thronged together, told the history, from his cradle to his grave of the peasant . . . A little higher up, with the faint horizontal line of the white cemetery-wall round it, and the vertical contour of tall poplars by its side [was] the red-tiled church.[1]

[1] *Winter's Tales*, New York, 1942, pp. 29–30.

In 'The Supper at Elsinore' the painter's eye is also clearly seen in the description of the winter-landscape along the coast-road between Copenhagen and Elsinore (a landscape she knew so well from her earliest days): 'Here and there seaweeds strewn upon the beach marked it with black and brown . . . The sky was the colour of lead, but low along the horizon ran a broad stripe the colour of old lemon peel or very old ivory.'[1]

One can see in these passages how the details have been organised into a deliberately arranged pictorial setting of contrasting colours exercising a strong aesthetic appeal in their line, colour and composition. Moreover, the fact that this is a conscious intention and one directed by a wider range of ideas is shown by the remarks that Isak Dinesen went on to make about art in the interview. After listing some of her tales directly influenced by a painting, she continued:

> I owe painting even much more. For it has constantly revealed the true nature of the real world to me. I have always had difficulty in seeing what a landscape really looked like unless I have been given the key to it by a great painter . . . Constable, Gainsborough and Turner have shown me England. As a girl, when I travelled in Holland, I understood everything that the landscape and the towns said because the old Dutch masters kindly acted as interpreters.

The attitude here is essentially an aesthetic one, and in reading these remarks one is struck by their similarity to those ideas expressed by Oscar Wilde, one of the chief exponents of aestheticism, in his dialogue 'The Decay of Lying':

> Life holds the mirror up to Art, and either reproduces some strange type imagined by a painter or sculptor, or realises in fact what has been dreamed in fiction . . . Things are because we see them, and what we see, and how we see it, depends on the Arts that have influenced us.[2]

The importance that she, like Wilde, attributes to art also provides a clue to the effect Isak Dinesen seeks to attain in her practice as a writer. A countryside is turned into a landscape, a

[1] *Seven Gothic Tales*, New York, 1961, p. 234.
[2] op. cit., *Poems and Essays*, London, 1956, pp. 258–259.

scene from real life is made into a work of art, and through this process the true nature of the real world is revealed.

Isak Dinesen also speaks about the impact made upon her by the lessons in perspective drawing which she attended as a student. This too reveals something which she was later to make a part of her general philosophy of life, but it also shows what her studies meant to her at the time:

> A new and beautiful aspect of the world revealed itself to me when I learnt perspective drawing . . . In a strange way I was carried away by its inflexible justice and laws. If I did things properly, the result was bound to be correct—but if I allowed myself the slightest negligence, it would wreak its revenge at the end of a problem, invariably, and with a terrible force.

In the light of this it comes as no surprise to learn that a discussion of the laws of perspective was once the grounds for a really violent disagreement between Isak Dinesen and her brother, Thomas, who is a trained engineer, for one can readily imagine how this way of expression could seem absurdly fanciful to someone trained in this field. But the imaginative stimulus which she derived even from studying perspective drawing, which so bored the other students, was probably the very reason why her studies appealed to her. In fact they offered an imaginative outlet additional to that which she found in her writing at this time.

Eventually, however, these, like her writing, failed to satisfy her completely, and she abandoned her course of formal studies at the Academy. All who knew her stressed that she was a perfectionist in everything she undertook, and in this fact almost certainly lies the main reason why she gave up: she realised that even if she had talent in this field, she certainly lacked anything more.

If this enterprise petered out, the social life she was leading did not bring her any lasting sense of achievement or satisfaction. She had reached an *impasse*. Thomas Dinesen has also stressed in conversation with me his sister's feelings of frustration during this stage of her life. She was trying, he thought, to keep up with a social set without having the financial means of really doing so, and to mix in the exclusive world of the Danish nobility of the time without having any definite place in its hierarchy. It is in fact possible to see her early life as torn between conflicting tendencies. On the one hand, she had the nature and dreams of an artist; on the other, with her spirited temperament, she was the daughter of a man who had lived an active and adventurous life, which represented an ideal for her. Some years later in Africa one of her friends told her that 'life will never make a tune for your dancing'.[1] It was seldom it did during these years in Denmark.

Of all her early writing perhaps the one which best sums up this phase of her life is a poem called 'Vinger' (Wings) which was only published posthumously. There is no indication in the manuscripts of the precise date of the poem, and Mr Dinesen was unable to say exactly when it was written, but had no doubt that it belonged to the period in Denmark, possibly when she was about eighteen. Written in Danish, it reads as follows when translated:

> In its prison my hearts sings
> Only of wings, only of wings.
> None of the world's lovely songs
> Echoes so sweetly to the ear.
> Even birds, born in a cage
> Soar freely in dreams to the skies,
> And in its prison my heart sings
> Only of wings, only of wings.
>
> High are the heavens, deep and limpid,
> A well of blue, sparkling with light.
> High will I soar without dizziness
> See the earth fade behind and sport with the winds.
> In summer the rose unfolds its buds
> And the world is wondrously beautiful.
> But in its prison my heart sings
> Only of wings, only of wings.

Although rather conventional in its imagery, there is still a

---

[1] Quoted by Aage Henriksen in *Det guddommelige Barn og andre Essays om Karen Blixen*, Copenhagen, 1965, p. 73.

certain poignancy in the poem; the emotions sound genuine enough, even if a little muffled by the vagueness of the language in which the dreams and their frustration, the hopes and their unfulfilment, are described. But this vagueness—the keynote of the poem—is also characteristic of its author's life at this time. Lacking a sense of fundamental purpose and a clear aim in life, Karen Dinesen was unable to define her aspirations and dreams more precisely in her poetry.

She did, however, retain these dreams; it is this fact which indicates the significance for her of the next stage of her life in Kenya. If the wings were only fully spread there, the longing to do so had been felt in Denmark. 'Life realises in fact what has been dreamed in fiction,' Oscar Wilde wrote. But Karen Dinesen had to wait until she lived in Kenya before her dreams materialised into fact to become the substance of her life there.

2

The African Years:
Baroness Karen Blixen

In 1913 Karen Dinesen became engaged to a Swedish cousin, Baron Bror von Blixen-Finecke. They had no cut-and-dried plans for the future, except that she was quite definite that she did not want to live on his family estate in Skaane, in the southern part of Sweden. An uncle of theirs happened to have recently returned from safari in East Africa, and his great enthusiasm for that country fired the young couple with the desire to emigrate there. The two families agreed to advance them money to buy a farm and, as she later put it, changing the motto, *navigare necesse est, vivere non necesse,* into 'it is necessary to farm, it is not necessary to live',[1] they made their decision to leave Denmark. Like her father some forty years previously, she too 'turned away from Europe and its civilisation'. The circumstances which led to this decision were quite fortuitous, and give ample confirmation to the remark that she made much later in life: 'When I was a young girl it was very far from my thoughts to go to Africa.'[2]

In January 1914 she and Bror Blixen were married in Mombasa. At first they went to live on a small farm and, shortly after, on a much larger one near Nairobi. This was to be Karen Blixen's home for the rest of her time in Kenya.

Her marriage was never a happy one. Mr Dinesen has told me that she and her husband had utterly different temperaments, and the measure of their divergent interests is perhaps sufficiently indicated by a remark she made in later years that Bror Blixen was a person who did not know whether the Crusades

[1] *On Mottoes of My Life,* Copenhagen, 1962, p. 19.
[2] *Paris Review,* p. 51.

dated from before or after the French Revolution. The differences between them, however, went very much deeper. Parmenia
Migel records that almost from the start of their marriage Karen
Blixen's husband was constantly unfaithful to her, and that she
caught a disease for which she had to return home for treatment.
Clara Svendsen and Frans Lasson are even more specific in
their biography:

> After the first year of marriage, Karen Blixen had to go home to
> Denmark to be treated for a venereal disease which she had con-
> tracted through no fault of her own. Too much time had elapsed
> before she set out; the journey took very long because of war con-
> ditions; and when she arrived in Denmark it took time to make dis-
> creet arrangements, which Karen Blixen insisted on, in order to
> keep her mother, with her Puritan upbringing, in ignorance of the
> situation. Karen Blixen herself believed that the long, hard years
> of illness she had to endure later in life were a result of this
> disease. It was with open eyes that she entered upon the same fate
> which she thought had threatened her father.[1]

The part that this must have played in influencing her whole
attitude to life needs no further elaboration.

Shortly after, Karen Blixen separated from her husband, and
in 1921 official divorce proceedings were instituted. Bror Blixen
subsequently made a name for himself as a big-game hunter
and safari-leader, with a wide circle of distinguished clients and
friends, including Hemingway. From the very beginning, big-
game hunting seems indeed to have preoccupied him much
more than the daily routine of running the farm. Some photo-
albums among Karen Blixen's papers, full of now-faded snap-
shots of the enormous variety of animals shot by him on safari
(either alone, or, in the early days, sometimes accompanied by
his wife) afford abundant testimony of this, and the account of
his experiences as a professional hunter was published in
English in 1937 entitled *African Hunter*. In 1946 he was killed
in a car accident in Sweden.

After their separation, Karen Blixen was left to run the farm
on her own. It was a large one and she had many Africans living

[1] *The Life and Destiny of Isak Dinesen*, p. 73.

on it both as servants and as squatters; these had to work on the farm for a certain number of days a year in return for holding some acres of land. In February, 1938, Karen Blixen gave a talk on the Danish radio in which she reckoned that there were about two hundred families of these squatters and that with women and children there were in all approximately two thousand people living on the farm. In some notes she made for a lecture in the same month, she remarked that it was really a feudal society, and this in regard both to the system of land tenure for the Africans and the prevailing spirit in the colony at the time is an accurate enough description. 'Life out there,' she once said, 'was, I believe, rather like eighteenth-century England: one might often be hard up for cash, but life was still rich in many ways.'[1]

There can be no doubt that it was. The sheer splendour of the country and her exhilaration in these new surroundings are so vividly recorded in the opening paragraphs of *Out of Africa* that they are worth quoting at some length. No shadow of adversity nor any hint of her illness is allowed to intrude to mar the effect:

> I had a farm in Africa, at the foot of the Ngong Hills. The Equator runs across these highlands, a hundred miles to the North, and the farm lay at an altitude of over six thousand feet. In the day-time you felt that you had got high up, near to the sun, but the early mornings and evenings were limpid and restful, and the nights were cold.
>
> The geographical positions, and the height of the land combined to create a landscape that had not its like in all the world. There was no fat on it and no luxuriance anywhere; it was Africa distilled up through six thousand feet, like the strong and refined essence of a continent. The colours were dry and burnt, like the colours in pottery ... Upon the grass of the great plains the crooked bare old thorn-trees were scattered, and the grass was spiced like thyme and bog-myrtle; in some places the scent was so strong, that it smarted in the nostrils ... The views were immensely wide. Everything that you saw made for greatness and freedom, and unequalled nobility.
>
> The chief feature of the landscape, and of your life in it, was the air. Looking back on a sojourn in the African highlands, you are

[1] *Paris Review*, p. 51.

struck by your feeling of having lived for a time up in the air . . .
Up in this high air you breathed easily, drawing in a vital assurance
and lightness of heart. In the highlands you woke up in the morning and thought: Here I am, where I ought to be.

One is struck by the similarity with the poem 'Vinger'—
except that now the vagueness of imagery and the mood of
aspiration have been replaced by an assured rendering of detail
and the expression of a profound sense of fulfilment. In the
Paris Review interview she said that as a girl she had never
dreamt 'that an African farm should be the place in which I
should be perfectly happy'. This is both true and untrue. The
decision to leave for Africa was indeed sudden and unforeseen;
on the other hand, she had dreamt as a child and young woman
—long and often. And in *Out of Africa* one can trace quite
unmistakeably the way in which her life there merges into the
world of her dreams:

> People who dream when they sleep at night . . . know that the real
> glory of dreams lies in their atmosphere of unlimited freedom . . .
> Great landscapes create themselves, long splendid views . . . All
> the time the feeling of immense freedom is surrounding him and
> running through him like air and light, an unearthly bliss.[1]

Poetry and dreams converge with life; the landscape of dreams is
made material as the surroundings of the farm at the foot of the
Ngong Hills and the cloudy imagining of the poetry has at last
been given a local habitation and name. Karen Blixen's life in
Denmark until the age of twenty-eight had really been a long
prelude to the years in Kenya, and without the previous sense
of confinement and frustration, her life there would neither
have seemed the liberation it did, nor would it have called forth
this elation in her.

What is also noteworthy about this is that, although she felt
this whole contrast so deeply, it is not one that figures in any
way as a main theme in her book. One has only to read the
following extract from the manuscript of an unpublished lecture
that she gave in 1938 to university students in Lund to become

[1] *Out of Africa*, New York, 1952, p. 87.

sharply aware of what has been omitted from her printed
work:

> Here at long last one was in a position not to give a damn for all
> conventions, here was a new kind of freedom which until then one
> had only found in dreams. It was like beginning to swim where one
> could stretch out in all directions, it was like beginning to fly
> where one seemed to have left the law of gravity behind. One
> might get a little dizzy, it was a little dangerous as well, it took
> courage, as it always does to recognise the truth. But it was
> glorious, intoxicating.

In fact one of the most striking things about *Out of Africa* is how
very little Karen Blixen does mention any details of her life
prior to Kenya and, even when they do occur, they consist of
only very fleeting and scattered references. 'My father was an
officer in the Danish and French army,' she notes on page 19,
for example, but it is not until some forty pages later that the
ambiguity of this remark is clarified and it is made clear what
nationality she actually was. Even then it is only very indirectly
stated with no further details: 'He was a countryman of mine, an
old blind Dane by the name of Knudsen,'[1] she starts, and
immediately continues, with nothing more about herself, but
instead with the unforgettable portrait of the old man.

Mr Dinesen, who actually spent over two years on the farm
with his sister, but who does not, by his own request, appear in
Out of Africa, once made a point about it in conversation.
Although it is true in all its details, he remarked, yet it is the
truth which has been seen through the eyes of an artist. It is a
point which gains additional substance from the fact that he was
speaking from personal experience of the life recorded in the
book and knew many of the people described.

In one way *Out of Africa* is a factual record—in Karen
Blixen's own words: 'When I write down as accurately as possible
my experiences on the farm, with the country and with some of
the inhabitants of the plains and woods, it may have a sort of
historical interest.'[2] On the other hand, it simply does not read

[1] *Out of Africa*, p. 56.
[2] ibid., p. 21.

like a straightforward recital of historical events or a diary of intimate experience. The book was started some five years after she had left Africa for good—like her tales therefore it deals with a period already set back in the past—and it consequently gains the quality that comes when the material is not one written up from immediate experience, but instead resides in completely assimilated memories long meditated upon. What happened is that during this lapse of time Karen Blixen was able to view her experiences with the selective eye of the artist, to sift the chaff from the grain, and to decide beyond any shadow of doubt what she wanted to include and—even more important—what to omit. And what is left out is every trace of intimate self-revelation and all the details of her previous life that would only distract the reader and blur the pristine clarity of the whole record of her encounter with Africa itself. In fact, a process of artistic selection operates just as rigorously in Karen Blixen's *Out of Africa* as in any of Isak Dinesen's tales.

Another area in which one can detect this winnowing process at work, besides the personal sphere, is in the account of the way of life of the European settlers in Kenya at the time. Some of the most fascinating records of this can be found in Elspeth Huxley's accounts of her early years in Kenya, *The Flame Trees of Thika* and *The Mottled Lizard*, and in her history of the colony, *White Man's Country*. Reading these one notices a fact that is not nearly so apparent in *Out of Africa*: if Kenya was not all things to all men, nevertheless it wore many different appearances. It could simply be an immense tract of wild country, ideal for big-game hunting and for safari; it could also contain farms established on a European pattern, modified somewhat to local conditions. It could be a place where near-feudal conditions pertained; it could offer conditions for the establishment of twentieth-century business enterprises; it could also provide a temporary resting-place for people, footloose, and unable to settle down anywhere for long. Settler life in the colony, as described in Elspeth Huxley's books, displays in fact a very much greater variety and embraces a much wider spectrum than one realises that it did from *Out of Africa*. One can take, for example, the following account of Nairobi, and

even if it, describes the town a few years before Karen Blixen
came to Kenya, there is no reason to believe that conditions
had greatly altered by then:

> Two or three times a year [Nairobi] would suddenly fill with sun-
> burnt, tattered settlers in broad-brimmed felt hats and revolver
> holsters. At such times there was something of an eighteenth-
> century spirit about the place. Aristocrats in fancy dress (or so
> their costumes would appear to a visitor fresh from England)
> paraded the streets or lounged over their drinks on the verandah of
> the Norfolk, which, on such occasions, came as near to achieving
> the atmosphere of a coffee-house as any hotel in Africa could.
> There was a certain robustness about evening carousals in the bar
> which carried on the traditions of the tavern.[1]

Kenya also seemed like eighteenth-century England to Karen
Blixen, but this cruder, more robust side of the 'aristocratic' life
receives no mention in her book.

One other example of the narrower and more highly selective
field covered by *Out of Africa* may be given. Lord Delamere,
one of the very first of the settlers and a founding father of the
colony, appears in Karen Blixen's book as an impressive, digni-
fied figure, a courtly, old-world English aristocrat. He was
undoubtedly that, but Elspeth Huxley reveals another and
totally unsuspected side to this picture:

> Delamere caused his friends a good deal of anxiety by joining in
> any rough-house he could find. . . . Once the manager of the
> Norfolk rashly approached him while he was acting as host at a
> dinner party to say that it was closing time . . . Delamere, in-
> furiated . . . said: 'Oh, damn the fellow, let's put him in the meat-
> safe.' He lifted the struggling manager bodily in his arms, carried
> him to the hotel meat-safe, locked him up with several dead sheep,
> and returned to the party.[2]

There is, however, one aspect of the life in Kenya that Karen
Blixen does dwell upon, and of which Lord Delamere was

[1] *White Man's Country. Lord Delamere and the Making of Kenya* (1935),
1953, Vol. I, p. 256.
[2] ibid., p. 256.

certainly a representative. Her attitude to the aristocracy has sometimes been the grounds for accusing her of snobbishness, even to the extent of suggesting that in this facet of her work is to be found one of the reasons for her popularity, especially in America.[1] It may well be that in her life there was a pronounced element of this; one notes, for instance, that she retained her husband's title throughout her life, and Parmenia Migel also offers a suggestion that something of this nature was one of the motives for her marriage in the first place.[2] If so, snobbishness is not an uncommon human failing, and the extent to which it was a potent factor in her whole life may be left to her biographer to determine. On the other hand, there is a side of this which does concern the literary critic. This snobbishness seems, on the face of it, to be transferred to the stories, where an admiration for the nobility of a hundred to a hundred and fifty years ago, and a wholehearted approval of aristocratic attitudes and behaviour are very apparent. But there are more fundamental reasons for this than mere snobbishness or nostalgia. 'I moved my stories back into a really romantic time,' she said in an interview given just after her first collection of tales had appeared, 'when people and conditions were different from today. I could become completely free only by doing this.'[3] The freedom she thus gained in art was only matched by that which she discovered in life by going to Kenya. There too she found conditions very different from the present.

The journey she made to Kenya was really one back in time, away from the twentieth century, to a country where the mode of life recalled that of the eighteenth. The clock there was not so much standing still—it had even been put back. In Denmark she had never truly been a member of the aristocracy, at most she was an outsider on the inside. The contrast in Kenya was striking indeed; there, immediately, and without question, she took up her position in an aristocratic hierarchy firmly based

[1] See *The Gayety of Vision*, p. 74, where Robert Langbaum gives examples of this type of criticism.

[2] 'What she kept to herself was her secret elation at . . . the consequent ties with Danish and Swedish aristocracy and the satisfaction of being addressed as "Baroness".' *Titania*, p. 40.

[3] *Politiken*, 1st May, 1934.

upon semi-feudal conditions. She was, she said, one of the 'May-
flower people', a member of the particular group of early settlers
who even had an insignia of their rank constantly in attendance.
This group 'might be characterised as those Europeans who
kept Somali servants . . . Here were Lord Delamere and Hassan,
Berkeley Cole and Jama, Denys Finch-Hatton and Bilea, and I
myself and Farah. We were the people who, wherever we went,
were followed, at a distance of five feet, by those noble, vigilant
and mysterious shadows.'[1]

In addition to this, the fact that all white settlers were living
in a colony conferred a special status upon them. It was one
most concisely summarised by Sir Edward Grigg, a governor of
Kenya during the nineteen-twenties:

> All white men and women destined to spend their lives in Africa . . .
> were born into a special and inalienable responsibility. Throughout
> their lives they would have to set a standard of civilisation among
> people still far behind them (whatever the future might hold) in
> culture. They were assigned to an involuntary aristocracy.[2]

Some of these involuntary aristocrats might, it is true, abuse this
position of responsibility (and evidence of this can also be found
in *Out of Africa* in the description of an African flogged to death
by his white employer[3]); but not Karen Blixen. The divergence
of her own views from many of the other settlers is shown by the
fact that she was at one time labelled 'pro-native'.[4] She regarded
her position as one exacting great obligations on her part. As
the landowner responsible for the people on the farm, she had
many duties to carry out as doctor, teacher, judge and counsellor.
Even after the farm had finally been sold, she devoted much time
and enormous energy to trying to ensure that the squatters on it
should be kept together, and when she succeeded in her efforts,
despite all her grief at leaving the farm, she was still able to
experience a feeling of deep contentment.

[1] *Shadows on the Grass*, New York, 1961, p. 17.
[2] Quoted in *White Man's Country*, Vol. II, p. 253.
[3] This section originally caused her some trouble with her publishers who
wanted it omitted. She refused.
[4] She mentions this in passing in 'Fra Lægmand til Lægmand' ('From
Layman to Layman'), one of the articles included in the collection, *Essays*,
Copenhagen, 1965, p. 99.

In our own day, it is easy to deride this attitude of *noblesse oblige* and dismiss it as anachronistic. That Karen Blixen did not share this view does not need saying; that she held to her conception of the responsibility conferred upon her with a passionate sense of dedication, however, does need stressing. This is one of her most fixed beliefs, made very apparent in *Out of Africa* and elsewhere. In the notes for the lecture given in February, 1938, she voiced this idea in the following terms:

> I loved the natives. In a way the strongest and the most incalculable emotion I have known in my life.
> Did they love me? No.
> But they relied on me in a strange, incomprehensible, mysterious way. A stupendous obligation. One would die for them. They took that quite for granted.

She expresses the same idea in a much lighter vein in the essay, *On Mottoes of My Life*. Quoting the verse,

> The great Emperor Otto
> Could never decide on a motto.
> He hovered between
> '*L'Etat c'est moi*' and '*Ich dien*,'

she says that her friend, Denys Finch-Hatton, used to tease her by saying that the first expressed her attitude to people of her own race, while the latter summarised her state of mind in dealing with the Africans. She adds that he was probably right.

This dedication to the ideal of *noblesse oblige*, and the whole concept of aristocracy bound up with it, cuts across all divisions of race and class. For Isak Dinesen in her tales, as well as for Karen Blixen in life, nobility recognises no social barriers. Her idea of aristocracy is represented just as faithfully by the Parisian music-hall dancer in 'The Heroine' as it is by the old nobleman in 'Sorrow-Acre'. In life, the ideal is embodied by many of the people depicted in *Out of Africa*, and includes not only men like Berkeley Cole and Denys Finch-Hatton (both of them English aristocrats), but also servants like Farah and Kamante, or people like the Kikuyu chief, Kinanjui, or even the whole warrior tribe, the Masai. All of these are aristocrats of the spirit; proud, fearless and noble, they represent those qualities in life that she most admired.

In *White Man's Country*, and again in *The Flame Trees of Thika*, Elspeth Huxley mentions a court case concerning a white settler in Kenya which took place in 1911 and caused much discussion at the time. The man was Galbraith Cole, the brother of one of Karen Blixen's closest friends in Kenya. For some time there had been numerous incidents of cattle and sheep stealing from his farm and the police seemed powerless to prevent this. Finally he took the law into his own hands. Finding three Africans skinning a stolen sheep, he arrested two of them and shot at the third and killed him while he was running away. He was put on trial for manslaughter and acquitted by a white jury, 'although the fact that he had shot the man was not denied. He claimed to have done so in defence of his property after he had appealed to the police and they had failed to protect him from continual robbery.'[1] The case received considerable publicity in England; there had been a similar one in Rhodesia a short time before when a white man had been acquitted by a white jury for shooting an African, and it was felt there had been a grave miscarriage of justice. Eventually, by direct order of the Secretary of State in London, Cole was deported.

These are the bare facts. How are they regarded by Karen Blixen? The case is not dealt with in *Out of Africa*, but she knew of it and referred to it in the lecture at Lund where she discusses the incident in some detail. After telling how Galbraith Cole caught the three Masai and shot one of them, she goes on to describe the trial:

> The judge said to Galbraith, 'It's not, you know, that we don't understand that you shot only to stop the thieves.' 'No,' Galbraith said, 'I shot to kill him. I had said that I would do so.' 'Think again, Mr Cole,' said the judge, 'we are convinced that you only shot to stop them.' 'No, by God,' Galbraith said, 'I shot to kill.' He was then sentenced to leave the country and, in a way, this really caused his death. But this case lived for a long time afterwards among the natives. I have often heard them talking about it

[1] *White Man's Country*, Vol. I, p. 281.

They called Galbraith Cole 'Debr Lao'. '"Debr Lao",' they would say, 'he had but one tongue in his mouth.' "Cattle die, kinsmen die, in the end we ourselves die. One thing I know that never dies: judgement on the dead."

The last sentences from the *Elder Edda* epitomise Karen Blixen's attitude and point to the major difference between the two accounts. For Elspeth Huxley as well as for the white settlers in Kenya and the authorities in England, the chief importance of the case lay in its political and legal aspects. What Karen Blixen, however, concentrates upon is the figure of Galbraith Cole. Having given his word that he would shoot, he had kept it and faced the consequences of his deed without any attempt to plead extenuating circumstances. For both writers, Cole is a man in a court of justice answerable to a system of law; but here the resemblance ceases: for Karen Blixen he also becomes an heroic figure obeying an epic code. How could a girl in this deadly boring twentieth century gain access to the heroic world? It was Kenya that provided the answer.

What we witness here is an example of a general attitude informing the whole of *Out of Africa*. The events and people depicted in the work are held together by a singleness of vision which invests them with an heroic dimension, while still retaining a basis of actuality; evaluates them in moral terms by assessing how far they adhere to this epic code of conduct; and selects and organises the details of daily life there to conform to this all-embracing vision.

This heroic ideal is one to which all people, black as well as white, may subscribe. It is this fundamental principle which lies behind much of Karen Blixen's attitude to the Africans, which is decidedly not established upon a set of political principles putting them on an equal, democratic footing with the whites. If Karen Blixen's attitude to the Africans is far removed from that shown by Elspeth Huxley in the very title of her book, *White Man's Country*, it is mainly because of this. With Karen Blixen there is even a predisposition in their favour because of their whole philosophy of life—one which obviously struck a deep chord of response in her. Commenting upon what she regarded as the Africans' utterly callous attitude to pain, Elspeth Huxley writes: 'In their eyes, I suppose, pain was simply a thing that had to be suffered'[1]; with Karen Blixen, this takes on an entirely different aspect:

> The Negro is on friendly terms with destiny, having been in her hands all his time; she is to him, in a way, his home, the familiar darkness of the hut, deep mould for his roots . . . in the face of pain . . . they generally showed little fear . . . They had real courage: the unadulterated liking of danger,—the true answer of creation to the announcement of their lot,—the echo from the earth when heaven had spoken.[2]

It is this heroic perspective of things that can be noted time and time again in the book. There is, for example, Kamante, the small Kikuyu boy, with his pitifully thin body and his legs from thigh to heel covered in deep running sores, who faces pain, so she thinks, with an heroic defiance that recalls Prometheus: 'Pain is my element as hate is thine. Ye rend me now: I care not. Ay, do thy worst. Thou art omnipotent.'[3] There are the Masai, the haughty warrior-tribe, with their memories of splendid battles and valiant deeds. There is Farah, ever attentive to her needs, faithfully serving his memsahib through all adversity, but retaining all the fiery pride and stubborn independence of the Somali tribe; or Old Knudsen, who believes in the legend of his mighty past, and dies still cherishing it. Many years later she was to make a remark that in all its simplicity defines better than anything else her attitude to the people depicted in *Out of Africa*. Talking about the great value friendship had had for her, she said, "I have been blessed with heroic friendships."[4]

All these heroic figures are displayed in a setting of equal splendour:

> It was lovely morning. The last stars withdrew while we were waiting, the sky was clear and serene but the world in which we

[1] *The Flame Trees of Thika*, London, 1962, p. 129.
[2] *Out of Africa*, pp. 23–24.
[3] ibid., p. 26.
[4] 'Isak Dinesen conquers Rome', *Harper's Magazine*, February, 1965, p. 49.

walked was sombre still, and profoundly silent. The grass was wet; down by the trees where the ground sloped it gleamed with the dew like dim silver ... The great vault over our heads was gradually filled with clarity like a glass with wine. Suddenly, gently, the summits of the hill caught the first sunlight and blushed. And slowly, as the earth leaned towards the sun, the grassy slopes at the foot of the mountain turned a delicate gold.[1]

The animals also take their allotted place in this array—not only the wild animals roaming the forests and plains, but even 'the noble and gracious' deerhounds living on the farm, or the young antelope, Lulu, who is described with such warm and quizzical humour. She condescends to make her home on the farm for a time and quickly subjugates the whole household to her slightest whim:

> ... my dogs understood Lulu's power and position in the house. The arrogance of the great hunters was like water with her. She pushed them away from the milk-bowl and from their favourite places in front of the fire. I had tied a small bell on a rein round Lulu's neck, and there came a time when the dogs, when they heard the jingle of it approaching through the rooms, would get up resignedly from their warm beds by the fireplace, and go and lie down in some other part of the room. Still nobody could be of a gentler demeanour than Lulu was when she came and lay down, in the manner of a perfect lady who demurely gathers her skirts about her and will be in no one's way.[2]

A lion-hunt with Denys Finch-Hatton is undertaken in the spirit of an epic enterprise. "Come now," she says to him, "let us go and risk our lives unnecessarily. For if they have got any value at all it is this that they have got none. *Frei lebt wer sterben kann.*"[3] They kill not one lion, but two, and the episode is wound up in the same spirit as it was begun with a few splendid sentences:

> We went back to the house and Juma brought and opened our bottle. We were too wet, and too dirty with mud and blood to sit

[1] *Out of Africa*, p. 73.
[2] ibid., pp. 70–71
[3] ibid., p. 232.

38

down to it, but stood up before a flaming fire in the dining-room
and drank our live, singing wine up quickly. We did not speak one
word. In our hunt we had been a unity and we had nothing to say
to one another.[1]

Denys Finch-Hatton, two years younger than Karen Blixen,
a son of the Earl of Winchilsea, educated at Eton and Oxford,
strikingly handsome and with great personal charm, was obviously very close to her, and although the full extent of her
feelings are never openly avowed, they are made very apparent
in the way she writes of him. 'Denys could indeed have been
placed harmoniously in any period of our civilisation, *tout
comme chez soi*, all up till the beginning of the nineteenth century. He would have cut a figure in any age, for he was an athlete,
a musician, a lover of art and a fine sportsman.'[2] Although this is
an intrusion into an aspect that she herself again treated with
reticence, one cannot avoid thinking that there may be a similarity between her relationship with him and one that is described in the unpublished story, 'Carnival'. In this, one of the
characters says about her husband that she is really deeply in
love with him, but she is desperately unhappy because, if he
knew what she felt, he would dislike it intensely. 'He wants me
to run parallel with him in life . . . I deceive him very well. I do
run parallel with him . . . I am his ideal friend and comrade,
and he believes that it is his car, and his aeroplane, and his
collections that I love. But it makes one sad always to deceive.'
This, of course, is only conjecture; but it is a fact that Thomas
Dinesen (who knew Finch-Hatton in Kenya) said that he was
the type of man who would never settle down anywhere;
marriage simply did not form part of his plans in life.

Elspeth Huxley, in another of her books on Africa, also bears
testimony to the attractiveness and charm of his personality.
She describes him as 'the legendary Finch-Hatton, a man never
forgotten or explained by his friends, who left nothing behind
him but affection, a memory of gaiety and grace', and she gives
an instance of his wit:

[1] *Out of Africa,* p 237.
[2] ibid., p. 215.

. . . once, when he was on safari in the very farthest, wildest regions, many days' march from contact with mails and telegraphs, a cable from London, forwarded from Nairobi by relays of runners with cleft sticks, caught up with him in the bush. Its content was brief. 'Do you know George Robinson's address?' Back went the reply as it had come, by relays of runners travelling for weeks with cleft sticks. It was even briefer. 'Yes.'[1]

The mere fact of his presence on the farm was sufficient to transform it for Karen Blixen:

When he came back to the farm, it gave out what was in it; it spoke,—as the coffee-plantations speak, when with the first showers of the rainy season they flower, dripping wet, a cloud of chalk. When I was expecting Denys back, and heard his car coming up the drive, I heard, at the same time, the things of the farm all telling what they really were. He was happy on the farm; he came there only when he wanted to come, and it knew, in him, a quality of which the world besides was not aware, a humility. He never did but what he wanted to do, neither was guile found in his mouth.[2]

Sometimes he would return unexpectedly while she was out in the fields supervising the work. Towards evening when she was due to return to the house, 'he would set the gramophone going, and as I came riding back at sunset, the melody streaming towards me in the clear cool air of the evening would announce his presence to me, as if he had been laughing at me, as he often did.'[3]

Shortly before her departure from Kenya, Finch-Hatton was killed when his plane crashed. She received the news at a luncheon-party in Nairobi, and, dazed with shock, she immediately returned home to make the preparations for the burial. Driving up into the hills in the mist of the dawn, she chose the site for the grave. In the early afternoon they brought the coffin out from Nairobi:

As it was placed in the grave, the country changed and became the setting for it, as still as itself, the hills stood up gravely, they knew

[1] *Forks and Hope. An African Notebook*, London, 1964, pp. 87–88.
[2] *Out of Africa*, p. 225.
[3] ibid., pp. 226–227.

and understood what we were doing in them; after a little while they themselves took charge of the ceremony, it was an action between them and him, and the people present became a party of very small lookers-on in the landscape . . . The clergyman . . . read out the funeral service . . . and in the great space his voice sounded small and clear, like the voice of a bird in the hills.[1]

After she had left Africa, she heard of a strange thing. At sunrise, and again at sunset, lions had been noticed coming to his grave: 'it was fit and decorous that the lions should come to Denys's grave and make him an African monument. "And renowned be thy grave." Lord Nelson himself, I have reflected, in Trafalgar Square, has his lions made only out of stone.'[2]

What is chiefly remarkable throughout this account is the controlled feeling, without a single false note, which ensures that a delicate equilibrium is maintained. This is the death and burial-ceremony of a hero; it is also the funeral of the man she loved. The event is endowed with heroic proportions without ever losing sight of the human perspective.

Finch-Hatton's death is indeed one of the emotional climaxes of *Out of Africa*; but the qualities of deep feeling in the way in which it is described are not restricted to this event. The warmth and sympathy communicated by *Out of Africa* has frequently been commented upon, and this is due in no small part to the way in which the figures who throng her pages are described. She displays an insight and understanding combined with a quick, imaginative sympathy which makes them come alive on the page and gives them a fully rounded quality. When one turns from these people to the characters in the tales, however, the contrast is a very marked one. The complexity is replaced by a rigid simplicity of outline, and the vividly coloured portraits in *Out of Africa* become mere black and white sketches with little or no shading. Even allowing for the fact that the short story cannot be the medium for full-scale, extensive exploration or detailed development of character, the differences still remain striking. And there is another aspect which makes the contrast even more puzzling. The figures in *Out of Africa* are not

[1] *Out of Africa*, pp. 356–357.
[2] ibid., pp. 360–361.

described at length throughout the course of the book, changing and developing as the book progresses—the technique in general of the novelist. They are really vignettes, seldom extending over more than a few pages. In its sharpness and economy, Karen Blixen's method of characterisation even in *Out of Africa* is essentially that of a short story writer.

The description of Berkeley Cole, another of her closest friends in Kenya, is typical of her method. He is described as a small, slight figure, red-haired, holding himself very erect, moving with all the silence and grace of a cat, and having its faculty of being able to make wherever he happened to be into a place of great comfort. 'When he was at his ease you expected to hear him purr, like a big cat, and when he was sick, it was more than sad and depressing, it was formidable as is the sickness of a cat.'[1] 'When he really chalked his soles for the job he was an inimitable buffoon,' but he could also carry a jest too far, and when he got on his high horse 'on the wall behind him the shadow of it began to grow and move, falling into a haughty and fantastical canter, as if it came of a noble breed and its sire's name had been Rozinante'.[2] Faithfully attended wherever he went by his Somali servant, Jama, he had once, he told Karen Blixen, lost his temper and hit him:

'... But then, my dear, you know,' said Berkeley, 'at the very same moment I had one straight back in my face.'

'And how did it go then?' I asked him.

'Oh it went all right,' Berkeley said, modestly. After a little while he added: 'It was not so bad. He is twenty years younger than me.'[3]

Something of a dandy, when staying on the farm he had a bottle of champagne brought out into the forest every morning at eleven o'clock, and once complained gently to Karen Blixen that he had not been given the best glasses for the occasion. He had a great love of the sea, and 'it was a favourite dream of his that he and I should,—when we had made money,—buy a dhow

[1] *Out of Africa*, p. 215.
[2] ibid., p. 214.
[3] ibid., p. 216.

and go trading to Lamu, Mombasa and Zanzibar.'[1] Like Finch-Hatton, he was, thought Karen Blixen, born out of his time: 'they were in reality exiles, who bore their exile with a good grace.'[2]

The fact that Karen Blixen so far in this character-portrait keeps very closely to life can be corroborated from Elspeth Huxley: 'Berkeley Cole was one of the old, colonial Kenya's legends, impossible now to pin down; a man whose brilliant colours faded, when he died, like those of a tropical fish or a blue-and-orange lizard. He had fine looks, supple conversation, grey eyes and a gay Irish wit. He never made money, entered politics, [or] took life seriously.'[3] But, with Karen Blixen, quite suddenly, one can see how the imagination seizes the pen in a few extra strokes that add another dimension to this portrait drawn from life. As well as remaining a living figure with small foibles and individualised features of personality, Berkeley Cole also becomes a type, one who has cropped up in many different periods of history:

> Berkeley, if he had had his small head enriched with a wig of long silky curls, could have walked in and out of the Court of King Charles II. He might have sat, a nimble youth from England, at the feet of the aged d'Artagnan, the d'Artagnan of *Vingt Ans Après*, have listened to his wisdom, and kept the sayings in his heart. I felt that the law of gravitation did not apply to Berkeley, but that he might, as we sat talking at night by the fire, at any moment go straight up through the chimney.[4]

Berkeley Cole is also of interest for another reason. One conjectures that some of the people Karen Blixen knew in real life served as models, even if greatly changed, for characters in Isak Dinesen's tales; in Berkeley Cole's case this can definitely be established. Moreover, the nature of the change he undergoes, very characteristic of her method in the stories, and one which is thrown into even sharper relief by the contrast it offers with that in *Out of Africa*, can also be traced. Amongst her manuscripts

[1] *Out of Africa*, p. 217.
[2] ibid., p. 214.
[3] *Forks and Hope*, p. 87.
[4] *Out of Africa*, p. 214.

there are several fragmentary drafts, a few pages in all, of a work described, like *Sandhedens Hævn*, as a 'marionette comedy'.[1] It is written in Danish and entitled *Elmis Hjerte* (Elmi's Heart). The action takes place in a villa in Mombasa and consists mainly of a conversation between the main character, suffering from a hangover caused by too much wine the previous evening, and a young girl. She sings to distract him, another character enters with the news that two ships have been sighted, probably pirates, making for Mombasa, and the fragment breaks off abruptly at this point. How it would have continued is now anyone's guess, but its chief interest lies in the names of the characters: Ali Hassan, an old slave-trader; Kamante, a boy; Abdullah, an old slave; Mira, an emissary from Somaliland; Elmi, Ali Hassan's nephew; and finally, Berkeley Cole, an Englishman and Elmi's friend. In addition to this draft there is also a typescript fragment, only three and a half pages in all, which is an English translation; and in this the name of Berkeley Cole has been changed to that of Lincoln Forsner, the main character in the tale, 'The Dreamers'.

When the two figures of Berkeley Cole and Lincoln Forsner are compared, one can see that they do have certain characteristics in common. Some of them are quite superficial. Lincoln Forsner is also the son of a rich family, he is red-haired, fond of the sea, and, when the story opens, he is sailing on a dhow from Lamu to Zanzibar—one of Berkeley Cole's favourite dreams. But in the story, the dreaming side of Berkeley Cole's nature has been made the central feature of Lincoln's character and the main-spring of his actions. Moved from life into the domain of

---

[1] There is no indication of the date of these drafts. Because of the setting and characters, however, it is virtually certain that they were written during the African years. Further evidence of this is provided by a small notebook, quite definitely used in Kenya, in which she jotted down some ideas for the story later to be published as 'The Dreamers'. Two of them can be quoted here in passing since they show how an idea was later woven into the fabric of the stories. One of them, written in Danish, reads in translation: 'The caliph gives the two lovers permission to be buried alive in the same coffin.' This becomes the anecdote related by the storyteller, Mira, in 'The Dreamers' (*Seven Gothic Tales*, pp. 273–274). The other, written in English, is only partly legible: 'What said Elmi is life but a . . . to turn a kitten into an old . . . a foal into a nag?' This forms the core of Lincoln Forsner's remarks in the same story (*Seven Gothic Tales*, p. 275).

art, the many-sided features of Berkeley Cole's personality have all been cut away at one stroke and attention is solely concentrated upon this single trait. Lincoln Forsner is a type, a dreamer —nothing more. In fact it would be impossible to guess, from reading this story only, that behind this figure stands Berkeley Cole, just as surely as the personality of Karen Blixen, with all the wealth of her experience in Kenya, stands behind Isak Dinesen.

Finally, in 1931, the life which Karen Blixen had spent in Africa came to an end. Already at the time of Berkeley Cole's death she noted that the country was changing. 'An epoch in the history of the Colony came to an end with him . . . now it was slowly changing and turning into a business proposition.'[1] The changes accelerated, and however desperately she tried to reverse the process, the farm slid deeper and deeper into debt. Confronted by these debts and by business worries wherever she turned, she resorted to the same means of distraction as in her earlier years. 'I began in the evenings to write stories, fairy-tales and romances, that would take my mind a long way off, to other countries and times . . . I used to sit and write in the dining-room, with papers spread all over the dinner-table, for I had accounts and estimates of the farm to do, in between my stories.'[2]

A few of these notebooks from the farm still survive and they offer a curious parallel to the exercise-books from the school-days at Rungstedlund. The harsher realities of life in the form of wage-bills and farm-accounts are all mixed up together with highly romantic ideas for stories, hastily scribbled down. At last, however, 'the business proposition' triumphed over everything, the farm was sold and, by a final irony, was eventually divided up into residential plots of land for Nairobi business people.

Karen Blixen's inconsolable grief when she was at last forced to leave is very apparent in the concluding section of *Out of Africa*, but at the same time, this is really only the overt expression of something that has been implied throughout. 'I *had* a

[1] *Out of Africa*, p. 223.
[2] ibid., pp. 44–45.

farm in Africa at the foot of the Ngong Hills': the end is fore-shadowed in the very first sentence. Nostalgia turns the pages of *Out of Africa*; the whole of it is written in the shadow cast by the title, and with an awareness, shared equally by the reader, that all this lies irrevocably in the past.

In ill-health, her closest friends dead, everything she had cherished in ruins, she returned to Denmark. Karen Blixen had taken the final step to becoming 'Isak Dinesen'.

3

The Latter Phase: 'Isak Dinesen'

During my first months after my return to Denmark from Africa, I had great trouble in seeing anything at all as reality. My African existence had sunk below the horizon. . . . The landscapes, the beasts and the human beings of that existence could not possibly to my surroundings in Denmark mean more than did the landscapes, beasts, and human beings of my dreams at night. Their names here were just words, the name of Ngong was an address . . . And here was I, walking in the fair woods of Denmark, listening to the waves of Øresund.[1]

Karen Blixen's life had swung full circle and she was back once more in her childhood home at Rungstedlund. But it was not only her 'African existence' that had disappeared; much else had gone besides. Europe of the early nineteen-thirties presented a very different picture from the pre-war world she had known as a girl. But the greatest changes of all had taken place, of course, within herself. She was now a woman of forty-six, and after the years spent in Kenya, she was really a totally different person. Her situation at this time is best described in her own words:

Now I was back again in my old home, with my mother, who received the prodigal daughter with all the warmth of her heart, but who did never quite realise that I was more than fifteen years old and accustomed, through the last eighteen years, to an existence of exceptional freedom. My home is a lovely place, I might live on there from day to day in a kind of sweet idyll, but I could not see any kind of future before me. And I had no money . . . I owed to the people on whom I was dependent to try and make some kind of existence for myself.[2]

[1] *Shadows on the Grass*, pp. 113–114.
[2] *On Mottoes of My Life*, p. 26.

She cast around for ways out of her predicament—some of them not without their more comic side. She asked her brother, Thomas, for instance, to finance her whilst she was training for some career; according to Parmenia Migel, when asked what sort of career she was thinking of, she pointed out that she had always had certain gifts for handling children and simple and backward people, so 'I believe I'd also succeed with the mentally deficient. Couldn't I train to be matron of an asylum?'[1]

A more obvious way, however, was open to her, even if it was not an easy one. 'Nothing,' Shelley wrote, 'is more difficult and unwelcome than to write without confidence of finding readers.' Living in Denmark, writing in English, Isak Dinesen could have no confidence at all. Nevertheless, she returned to the stories she had already started working upon during the last months in Kenya.[2] Revising these and writing others, she completed a collection, and after having been rejected several times, it was eventually accepted for publication in America in 1934. It also appeared in England in the same year.

As if to show that she was putting her former life behind her and making a fresh start, she adopted a pseudonym. It was quite easy to do this in England and America, but in Denmark, a much smaller and more closely-knit community, it was not long before the identity of the author behind the pseudonym was tracked down. At the time she was very resentful that this had happened and she voiced this resentment publicly some years later. Subsequently, however, she had to accept that the secret of her pseudonymous identity had been discovered in Denmark, and she used the name of Karen Blixen for all her later works published there.

[1] *Titania*, p. 92.
[2] There is some doubt how many stories she actually wrote in Kenya; Thomas Dinesen says that when he met his sister in Marseilles on her return to Europe, she read *three* of them aloud to him one evening. He was considerably impressed by them, but she said that they would have to be thoroughly worked over again. In *Mottoes of My Life* (p. 26) Isak Dinesen herself says, quite specifically, that she wrote *two*. No drafts of these stories survive among the MSS, so it is impossible to confirm this from that source. The explanation is probably that some of the stories were written in Kenya and then revised, or even entirely rewritten. Corroboration of this could be found in the later MSS, where it is obvious that her practice was to revise her stories over and over again before final publication.

That the original intention behind the use of a pseudonym was more than a mere whim became quite apparent some ten years after this. In 1944 a novel called *Gengældelsens Veje* was published in Denmark, and the name of the author was given as Pierre Andrézel.[1] The book has little or no value as literature; interest soon centred upon the author's identity, and it was not long before the book was attributed to Isak Dinesen. In reply she wrote a newspaper article, in which she said that even if she were the author, she would on no account acknowledge the book as hers, and added that it was quite obvious that it had simply been written as mere entertainment.[2] However, the chief interest of this article lies in a remark which she made about the use of pseudonyms in general. 'A pseudonym,' she wrote, 'is not a deception; it is a mask.'[3] 'Isak Dinesen' not only marks a new departure in her life; it establishes a *persona*.

We have already noted the revolution in her life brought about by the move to Kenya; the publication and subsequent success of *Seven Gothic Tales* also marked another great turning-point. There is, however, one major difference: the stage Isak Dinesen embarked upon when she became a professional writer, the adoption of a pseudonym to denote this, together with the conditions which this imposed upon her life, were all the result of a wholly premeditated decision taken in response to the new situation. In the same way that many artists create a myth which shapes the way they live, Isak Dinesen, quite deliberately, fashioned a mask.

In *Out of Africa* she refers frequently to the wealth of entirely new experiences and the sense of revelation which the encounter with the Africans gave her, although she nowhere defines the nature of this experience in more precise terms. Amongst her unpublished papers, however, there is a crucial passage which

[1] It appeared in England in 1946 with the title *The Angelic Avengers*; the author's name remained unchanged.

[2] It was not until the *Paris Review* interview in 1956 that she finally acknowledged she was the author. In *Shadows on the Grass*, she described how she had written it as a distraction during the German occupation of Denmark, and added firmly, if playfully, that she regarded it as 'a highly illegitimate child'.

[3] The article from *Politiken* is reprinted in Hans Brix's study, *Karen Blixens Eventyr*, Copenhagen, 1949, pp. 254–257.

both defines this and which also further illustrates the significance of her pseudonym. In the course of the lecture she gave in Lund, she made the following comments:

It may happen to some of you, you young Swedish men, whom I am addressing this evening, that you will travel to distant lands, unknown to you. I can tell you that this will be a strange experience for you. You will find that not only will your surroundings change and be strange and unknown wherever you turn, but that you yourselves will change in your own eyes so that you will eventually ask the question, 'Who am I? What do I look like?'

As long as you are a child at home, this question does not arise, all your surroundings can answer it; they are in agreement and their common judgement usually affords the basis of the evaluation we make of ourselves. And as long as you remain in your native country, you are in a sense at home, all the people you meet there have approximately the same background. . . .

But one day you come to a people who see us with different eyes. Even if you learn their language, they won't have the same kind of ear you are used to addressing. If you tell them that you come from Lund, it will mean nothing at all to them . . . If you tell them that your father is a managing director or a bishop or a general, it won't mean anything to them because they don't know what a director or a bishop or a general is . . . They won't even know that you are polite when you raise your hat, and well-dressed when you are in tails.

And while you are divesting yourselves, in a way, of your social and intellectual attitudes one by one, it will slowly dawn upon you that, after all, these may not have constituted your true being, and that something remains behind when they disappear. Who am I then, since I am no longer the same person I have previously been taken for? Then the truest answer must be: a human being. Simply and solely as a human being you meet the black, primitive people.

This experience was for me a kind of revelation, not only of the world, but also of myself. And I can say that it was a great and unexpected happiness, a liberation . . . one more step in this direction, I thought, and then I will be face to face with God.

After this experience she was back again in Europe. All the conditions which enabled her to find her true self with the Africans and almost 'stand face to face with God' had disappeared. In her own country once more, 'in a sense at home'—

even if a greatly altered one—compelled to make 'some kind of existence' for herself, faced with the impossibility of again putting on the social and intellectual attitudes of which she had divested herself so thoroughly, she chose another course. 'Who am I? What do I look like?' And for answer this time she donned the mask of 'Isak Dinesen'.

What were the main features of her mask? What was its expression? One does not need to look far in order to find the answer: the mask is the one created by her work. With her the style is not the man—it is the mask; the life assumes the characteristics of a literary artifact, and the mask of Isak Dinesen is the public face worn in a public place.

The particular form, which the relationship between the writer's life and his art took with Isak Dinesen, is not, of course, unique. With Byron, for example, one can also trace a similar process, in which Byron the man assumes the mask of the Byronic figure, and, in public, lives up to the legend depicted in the verse tales and in *Childe Harold*—even though there is plenty of evidence in his letters that in private he could be a very different person. It seems no coincidence, therefore, that Byron is mentioned several times in Isak Dinesen's work and that one of the best of her unpublished stories, 'Second Meeting', has him as a main character. Another case in point is Oscar Wilde; even though, unlike Byron, he identified himself so completely with the Wildean figure, and carried out the process of life imitating art to such an extent that he could even feel that it was into life he had put his genius and only his talents into his work: 'I treated art as the supreme reality and life as a mere mode of fiction.' This certainly represents an extreme, but it also expresses an aesthetic creed very close indeed to Isak Dinesen's own attitude to art and to her mode of life after assuming the artist's vocation. Nevertheless, in the case of both Wilde and Byron, the writer's life follows a pattern exemplified by a particular character that occurs again and again in their work. A Wildean figure exists just as surely as does a Byronic hero. This is not the same with Isak Dinesen. There is no Dinesen main character in the tales, with whom the author identifies herself, nor was there, presumably, the same psychological motivation urging her to project the inner self in this way as there probably was in Byron's case, and certainly was in Oscar Wilde's. Isak Dinesen assumed a mask in order to fill the emptiness she found in her environment in Denmark, and created an artistic conception of herself to replace the identity of which circumstances had robbed her. The writer she has even closer affinities to in this respect is W. B. Yeats. 'Style, personality—deliberately adopted and therefore a mask—is the only escape from the hot-faced bargainers and the money-changers.'[1] If style and personality are synonymous terms with both, if Isak Dinesen shares with Yeats an aristocratic disdain for business and 'the business proposition', so too is the means of escape the same.

In a memoir of the Irish writer, AE, by John Eglinton, a letter about Yeats, written by AE, analysing his character, is quoted:

> He began about the time of *The Wind among the Reeds* to do two things consciously, one to create a 'style' in literature, the second to create or rather to recreate W. B. Yeats in a style which would harmonise with the literary style. People call this posing. It is really putting on a mask, like his actors . . . a mask over life. The actor must talk to the emotion on the mask, which is a fixed emotion. W. B. Y. began twenty years ago vigorously defending Wilde against the charge of being a poseur. He said it was merely living artistically, and it was the duty of everybody to have a conception of themselves, and he intended to conceive of himself. The present W. B. Y. is the result . . . He has created the mask and he finds himself obliged to speak in harmony with the fixed expression of the mask.[2]

As 'Isak Dinesen' Karen Blixen also recreated herself in a style of life harmonising with the literary style, and a glance at her work will indicate its nature. For, although it remains true that there is no Dinesen figure in the tales as a main character, like Childe Harold, for example, or Lord Illingworth, there is still one person who is present in every single story—the storyteller herself. In reading Isak Dinesen one receives a quite indelible impression of the *persona* of the narrator, always present as a

[1] W. B. Yeats: *Autobiographies*, London, 1955, p. 461.
[2] *A Memoir of AE: George William Russell*, London, 1937, pp. 110–111.

kind of reflective intelligence, speculating, describing, narrating, commenting, but doing all these things with a curious air of aloof detachment—curious, because there is abundant evidence from people who knew Isak Dinesen personally that she was utterly different from this in private life. Although a highly unusual, even strange person at times, she was also a gay, witty, charming woman with a compelling personality, possessed of great gifts of warm sympathy and understanding. But in her tales, the sense of distance is maintained throughout, and even deliberately cultivated by her steadfast refusal ever to identify herself overtly with any of her characters or to sympathise with their actions by explicit comment. This effect of studied detachment is a crucial element in her writing; it is one which is further strengthened by the technique; and it is worth pausing for a moment to consider it in a little more detail.

By means of this technique we are kept continually aware of the fact that we are reading a story, and this is often further emphasised by one of her favourite devices of including a story within a story. A clue to the deeper significance of this technique is provided by some remarks that Henry James made. In affirming his cardinal belief that the writer must relate events that are assumed by the reader to be real, and that this illusion of presenting reality is one that must be preserved at all costs, James deplores the fact that Trollope 'took a suicidal satisfaction in reminding the reader that the story was only, after all, a make-believe. He habitually referred to the work in hand (in the course of that work) as a novel, and to himself as a novelist.'[1] Isak Dinesen also constantly refers to her work as a story and herself as a storyteller, and if this was suicidal, then she committed suicide in every story she ever wrote. Like Trollope, her stories never take any pains to preserve the illusion of reality; they, too, are always a matter of make-believe, of 'once upon a time . . .' Tales made up for the occasion, they are told by a storyteller, and these facts are everywhere openly acknowledged and firmly underlined. And if Trollope constantly administered what Henry James, rather nicely, describes as 'these little slaps

[1] 'Anthony Trollope' in Henry James. *The Future of the Novel*, edited by Leon Edel, New York, 1956, p. 247.

at credulity', Isak Dinesen imperiously ignores any demand that credulity should be the effect striven for at all.

In addition to this, as readers, we are never made contemporaries of the characters in time, in the sense of living through the story's action, side by side with them. Knowing all the while that this is a story, we are not so much made aware what is happening, as told what *has* happened. Isak Dinesen's tales are not meant as a representation of events taking place in time according to the way things happen in life; instead they are accounts of what has already taken place. Consequently, they are narrated, not in response to the demands of realistic presentation, but according to the dictates of artistic exposition and the requirements of their structural arrangement. In short, they are not organised as an imitation of life; instead, they preserve an unapproachable distance from it—like their author.

One final point remains to be touched upon. The viewpoint from which the tales are narrated is, of course, that of the omniscient author, the method Henry James was criticising so strongly. But Isak Dinesen uses this in a way that immediately sets her apart from many other writers. In her stories the omniscient author is present all the time, but not, however, as an individualised personality who creates a close human relationship with his reader—the type of relationship which one finds, for example, in Fielding or E. M. Forster. On the contrary the reader is kept very firmly in his place, while she maintains hers; Isak Dinesen, in fact, carries on a dialogue in which the chief auditor is herself. Far from there being any direct appeal or address to the reader, an effect is given that he is almost *overhearing* a story told aloud, while the author studiously ignores his presence.

That this unapproachability is a fully conscious attitude, indeed a carefully sought effect, is made clear by 'The Cardinal's First Tale', one of her later stories. It is the one which comes as near as any of her tales to being an open confession of her creed as a writer, and it is directly engaged with the problem of the artist's identity. It starts by posing the question: '"Who are you?" the lady in black asked Cardinal Salviati.'" In reply, the Cardinal says, '"I am not in the habit of talking about myself, and your demand makes me feel a little shy . . . But . . . I am beginning to take an interest in your question. Allow me, then . . . to answer you in the classic manner, and to tell you a story." "[1]

His mother bore identical twins. The parents could not agree on what vocation each of the boys should follow; one of them was intended for the priesthood by his father, while the mother decided the other was to be an artist. But shortly after their birth, one of them perished in a fire. The question is: which one really was saved? Even the Cardinal is not certain of his true identity, and nothing in his life can enlighten him, since both artist and priest share a common fate. ' "Who is the man," he asks, "placed on earth . . . because he is God's mouthpiece, and through him the voice of God is given forth? Who is the man who has no existence of his own—because the existence of each human being is his?" '[2]

Among Isak Dinesen's manuscripts there is a note in which the germ of this story can be found:

> The boy who is one of two twins [sic]—one of them intended by one of the parents to be a priest; the other to be a *bon viveur* (an artist? merchant?). The parents can only distinguish the one from the other when they see them together. One of them falls out of a window and is killed—(is run over, perishes in a burning house?) and he does not even know himself whether he is his brother or himself. (They are christened, one named after an especially ascetic saint, the other after—Casanova? Louis XV?) The different attitudes to life of the parents and their quarrel about the children.

The note shows how the implications of Isak Dinesen's tales can grow and develop in the process of writing. Hardly a hint can be gathered from this of the sacerdotal nature of the artist's vocation, so strongly brought out in the finished tale; there is even the suggestion that the artist might instead be either a merchant or a *bon viveur*. On the other hand, it does show, even at this preliminary stage, that the fact that the Cardinal himself does not know his own identity is to be a main theme. This again

---

[1] *Last Tales*, pp. 3–5.
[2] ibid., pp. 20–21.

develops into something not found in the original idea—the concept of the story and the relationship of the storyteller to his audience.

The lady's reply to the story she has heard is significant:

> 'Your Eminence,' she said, 'in answer to a question, has been telling me a story, in which my friend and teacher is the hero. I see the hero of the story very clearly, as if luminous even, and on a higher plane. But my teacher and adviser—and my friend—is farther away than before. He no more looks to me quite human.'[1]

In a way the lady is here echoing the general reaction of Isak Dinesen's readers to her stories—and the author herself knows this full well. The story shows how deliberately the distance between the reader, on the one hand, and the artist-narrator, on the other, is maintained, and how consciously the impersonality and aloofness of the artist are adopted and even insisted upon. It has, however, a further significance when placed in the context of the discussion here. 'Who am I? What do I look like?'—and instead of answering the question by directly describing his own character and personality, the narrator refers the questioner back to the *story* for an answer. It is by actually telling a story, by creating a work of art, that the artist establishes his identity—such as it is.

But there is also another way in which the narrator's presence is made very apparent in Isak Dinesen's work. It lies in the consistency and uniformity of tone preserved throughout, and the formal, mandarin prose-style in which the stories are written. Isak Dinesen's prose-style must be one of the most distinctive in English, and is as easily recognisable as, say, that of such utterly different writers as Hemingway or Henry James. It is, in every sense of the word, a literary style, very far removed indeed from ordinary colloquial speech, and from any consequent associations with everyday life, and thus serving to accentuate even more the flight of imagination from daily life which the contents describe. Practically any passages could be chosen to illustrate this; the following are typical. The Cardinal, in 'The Deluge at Norderney', addresses his companions,

[1] *Last Tales*, p .23.

marooned with him by the floods in the hay-loft, in these terms:

> 'Still, Madame, has not the Lord arranged for us here a day of judgement in miniature? It will be soon midnight. Let it be the hour of the falling of the mask. If it be not your mask, or mine, which is to fall, let it be the mask of fate and life. Death we may soon have to face, without any mask. In the meantime we have nothing to do but to remember what life be really like. Come, Madame, and my young brother and sister! As we shall not be able to sleep, and are still comfortably seated, tell me who you are, and recount to me your stories without restraint.'[1]

One notes the deliberate archaicisms here: 'If it be not your mask, or mine'; the sentence inversion: 'Death we may soon have to face'; and the formality of 'recount to me your stories without restraint'. This is a highly mannered prose, level, composed—in every sense of the word, seldom varying in tone. And Miss Malin's mode of speech in the same story does not differ noticeably from the Cardinal's:

> 'And now, what, My Lord,' said the old lady, 'do you think of womanly modesty? Surely, that is a divine quality; and what is it but deceit on principle? Since here a youth and a maiden are present, you and I, who have observed life from the best of observatories— you from the confessional, and I from the alcove—will take pains to disregard the truth; we will talk only of legs. I can tell you, then, that you may divide all women according to the beauty of their legs. Those who have pretty legs, and who know the concealed truth to be sweeter than all illusions, are the truly gallant women, who look you in the face, who have the genuine courage of a good conscience. But if they took to wearing trousers, where would their gallantry be?'[2]

The characters do not use individualised speech-rhythms; in this sense they are, all of them, really *personae* of the author through whom she herself speaks. One comparison of this passage with another on something of the same subject, must suffice to illustrate this. Herr Soerensen, the old actor and

---

[1] *Seven Gothic Tales*, p. 27.
[2] ibid., p. 25.

theatre-director in 'Tempests' is described in this way:

> He would also, in exuberant pride and joy, give her a few fatherly taps on her behind and then, more to himself than to her, develop his theories upon female beauty.
>
> 'How many women,' he said, 'have got their tails where they ought to be? In some of them—God help them—they are coming down to their heels! You, ducky,' he added cheerfully with his cigar in his mouth, 'are long in the leg! Your trotters don't pull you downwards—Nay, your two legs are straight and noble columns —which proudly carry, where you walk or stand—your whole nice little person heavenwards!'[1]

This is something which—fortunately—does not happen often, 'Your trotters don't pull you down'; if this is the attempt to make him speak in character, it is also Isak Dinesen writing very much *out* of character. The authentic Isak Dinesen accent, which speaks through her persons and imparts its typical quality to the whole story, can be found in the parenthesis: 'Nay, your two legs are straight and noble columns.' The tone, emanating directly from the author, reveals the style of an artist who carefully weighs every word, calculates their every effect, and deliberately fits them into their allotted places as parts of an ordered whole.

If Flaubert's dictum that the artist must be in his work as God is in creation, invisible, but all-powerful, sensed everywhere, but seen nowhere, represents one pole of narrative technique, then Isak Dinesen's must be placed at the opposite. The technique in her stories is not only that of the omniscient author, but that of an author who knows everything because she is present everywhere, seen everywhere, expressing everything in her own unmistakable manner, and never failing to remind us of her presence by the distinctive, highly personal idiom in which the stories are couched. It is a style, not spontaneous, but measured, not natural, but highly artificial—a style deliberately directed to the purpose of showing the reader the unreality of her world of fiction and of how little like ordinary life it is. And the same features can be traced in her later life.

---

[1] *Anecdotes of Destiny*, New York, 1958, p. 88. Since this story is an exception to her usual practice in being first written in Danish, one should add that the incongruity is equally great in that language.

Only a brief indication of these features can be given here, even though one is tempted to treat this aspect more fully, since it exercises a good deal of fascination. For what one witnesses is the contrast between Karen Blixen's life, with all its richness, variety and warmth of personality on the one hand, and the public *persona* of 'Isak Dinesen', distant and unapproachable, on the other. The writer begins where the woman ends. 'Not by the face shall the man be known, but by the mask,' one of her characters says,[1] and this is also true of his author. There exists evidence of this in a portrait of her painted in 1955 by a Danish artist, Kay Christensen. A highly unusual writer with a strange personality has inspired a deeply imaginative portrait, and the painter has brilliantly responded to the challenge of his subject. He has not only painted her as she appeared in life, he has also managed to convey something of the aura she created around herself as a writer. The outline of her figure is sketched in with the briefest of detail so that attention is concentrated on the face, depicted as a white mask, with the eyes, dark, sunken and compelling, accentuating the atmosphere of enigma and mystery. The portrait is, quite recognisably, that of Karen Blixen; but the sibylline features are those of Isak Dinesen.

Additional evidence of these same features can be found. There is, for instance, the mask-like quality of impersonality and of detachment from the present day implied in the remark once made about her, which she loved to quote, that she was really three thousand years old and had dined with Socrates. And in spite of the rather breathless style, Eugene Walter also conveys something of the impression she made of a person remote from ordinary existence and humanity:

> ... the Baroness Blixen, known also as Tania, as Karen, was quite simply, the most fascinating human being I have ever met ... Her face was very slim ... It was a mercurial face, an eager face, a timeless one ... Here was some eternal human mystery crystallised in a ninety-pound Danish lady, of any age you might care to guess. A sybil.[2]

[1] *Seven Gothic Tales*, p. 175.
[2] *Harper's Magazine*, February, 1965, p. 47.

In New York, during the winter 1958–59, she gave a public reading of her stories, and another description of the effect she made by her public *persona* is found in Glenway Wescott's *Images of Truth*:

> ... she established herself in an important straight chair, spot-lit, and after catching her breath in physical weariness for a moment, and gazing around the auditorium ... began the evening's narration. She has an ideal voice for the purpose, strong, though with a kind of wraithlike transparency, which she is able to imbue with emotions, but *only narrative emotions* ... What especially colors Isak Dinesen's voice, what gives it overtone and urgency, is remembrance or reminiscence ... *not perturbed* by her listeners, perhaps even helped by them, she seems to be *re-experiencing* what she has to tell, or if it is fable or fantasy, *redreaming* it.[1]

Finally, the way in which she herself saw her public *persona* and the aura surrounding it, is given most clearly in some remarks which she made on the record when introducing two extracts from her stories:

> I belong to an ancient, idle, wild and useless tribe, perhaps I am even one of the last members of it, who, for many thousands of years, in all countries and parts of the world, has, now and again, stayed for a time among the hard-working honest people in real life, and sometimes has thus been fortunate enough to create another sort of reality for them, which in some way or another, has satisfied them. I am a storyteller.[2]

'A storyteller'; this was the *persona* she assumed and the mask she donned in public.

We have already noted a degree of similarity between the *persona* of Isak Dinesen and Yeats's doctrine of the mask. Professor Ellmann, in his excellent study, *Yeats: The Man and the Masks*, offers one of the most lucid accounts of this doctrine in which further similarities can be observed. Remarking that it is one which has multiple meanings for Yeats, he goes on to dis-

---

[1] Glenway Wescott: *Images of Truth. Remembrances and Criticism*, London, 1963, p. 151. My emphasis.

[2] *Karen Blixen fortæller* ... (Lousiana Grammofonplader).

tinguish some of them. In its simplest form, the mask is the social self (one thinks of Eliot's Prufrock reflecting that 'there will be time to prepare a face to meet the faces that you meet'), it includes, in fact, 'all the differences between one's own and other people's conception of one's personality. To be conscious of the discrepancy which makes a mask of this sort is to look at oneself as if one were somebody else.'[1]

The effect of alienation, suggested here, is a precise description of Karen Blixen's traumatic experience in Africa: made to see herself through the eyes of the Africans, she too began to look at herself as if she were another person. But the parallel with Yeats does not cease here. The mask, Ellmann says, 'is a weapon of attack; we put it on to keep up a noble conception of ourselves; it is a heroic ideal which we try to live up to'.[2] If this is the foundation upon which Yeats established his concept of pride, 'bound neither to Cause nor to State', and the source of the heroic, inhuman quality with which he invested it, (casting 'a cold eye on life, on death'), Isak Dinesen also had a very similar ideal. In a sense, the motto affixed to *Out of Africa*, *Equitare, Arcum tendere, Veritatem dicere*, changes its character when applied to the life she created by means of her fiction. She turned away from the active life to the artist's calling—but still retained the heroic ideal which had dominated the early stages. Now, however, this is transferred from the plane of real life ('the hard-working honest people of real life') to that of art and the artist ('another sort of reality'). The artist becomes, in her eyes, a proud and noble figure, dedicated to a lonely existence, alienated from life precisely because he is an artist, and striking an heroic attitude amidst his isolation. Again one thinks of the affinity with Byron.

Another function of the mask for Yeats was to act as a guard, either against overmuch introspective analysis of the Soul by the Self, or as a means of defence to shield the real face from the public gaze. Protected by this, detached and aloof from any hurt, we are less involved in what may happen to us, either

[1] Richard Ellmann; *Yeats: The Man and the Masks*, London, 1961, pp. 175–176.
[2] *ibid.*, p. 176.

through external circumstances or by wounds inflicted from within:

> I think that all happiness depends on the energy to assume the mask of some other self; that all joyous or creative life is a rebirth as something not oneself, something which has no memory and is created in a moment and perpetually renewed. We put on a grotesque or solemn painted face to hide us from the terrors of judgement, invent an imaginative saturnalia where one forgets reality, a game like that of a child, where one loses the infinite pain of self-realization.[1]

Isak Dinesen also invented an imaginative world in which one can forget reality and lose the infinite pain of self-realisation; once she remarked that all sorrows can be borne if they are put into a story, or a story is told about them. She would in fact have been able to subscribe whole-heartedly to Eliot's dictum of the impersonality of art when he proclaimed that 'poetry is not a turning loose of emotion, but an escape from emotion; it is not the expression of personality, but an escape from personality'. It becomes clear, really, that however isolated Isak Dinesen felt herself as a writer, however strange and singular her work seems on the surface to the modern reader, nevertheless, in its central aspect of detachment and impersonality—even though caused by circumstances of life peculiar to herself—it is really very much in tune with other writers of the age. This is not, however, to postulate a direct influence; *her* route was a very different one, even if the destination turned out to be the same.

The idea that sorrows become bearable when transmogrified into art, by making up a story about them, is one which occurs frequently in her work. ('We're lucky,' as Philip Roth expressed it, 'nothing truly bad can happen to us. It's all material.') Both 'The Dreamers' and 'Echoes', for instance, illustrate this concept, and 'The Young Man with the Carnation' and 'A Consolatory Tale' contain a similar idea, expressed in more general terms, of how much of life the artist is forced to renounce. All these stories, moreover, are related, if indirectly,

[1] *Autobiographies*, pp. 503–504.

to Isak Dinesen's own life; the way this is so can be seen much more directly in an unpublished story called 'Second Meeting'.

This is a later story (one typescript draft is headed 'Tales from Albondocani'; 'Chapters from the Novel Albondocani' form part of *Last Tales*), and it exists in a finished, but unrevised form, among her manuscripts. One of the two main characters is Byron. The other is called Giuseppino Pizzuti, nicknamed Pippistrello, who also figures in 'Of Hidden Thoughts and of Heaven' and in 'Night Walk', both in *Last Tales*. Among the working-notes for this story, she made one to show the major idea underlying her conception of him and how she intended to develop this. It is a note that points unerringly to the way in which Pizzuti mirrors her own situation, and to the connection, otherwise carefully concealed from view, between the mask of Isak Dinesen, on the one hand, and the living woman and the different lives she had lived, on the other. 'Pippistrello tells how he lost his own life, but gained instead a great many stories. The joy and the sorrow of having many lives.' The story elaborates this theme.

A meeting takes place between Byron and Pizzuti, the owner and director of a marionette theatre, in Byron's palazzo in Genoa on the eve of his departure for Greece. Pizzuti tells him that fourteen years ago Byron had saved his life, and relates how this had happened. At that time they were both living on Malta, and he had heard of a plot to kidnap Byron and kill him. Since Pizzuti had always admired him and, moreover, resembled him to a striking degree, he had decided to impersonate him and to save his life in this way. He had been kidnapped, and the bandits, upon learning of their mistake, had informed Byron of what he had done and demanded a ransom for him. He had sent them a sovereign in jest, and Pizzuti was released. Now that he had heard of his imminent departure, he had decided to visit him since '"it was", I reflected, '"the last moment to show you what kind of life it is that you have saved".' He then goes on to say that it is really Byron who is responsible for his life as a director of a marionette theatre since the bandits had presented him with the sovereign they had received as a ransom:

'With that I started my marionette theatre, which has since flourished . . . and has made me famous in Italy. If you had come to see my theatre, you would have found out there, what you had bought, for everything that has happened to me since, I have turned into a story. That has been my life.'

'For I shall tell you,' he went on, 'in accepting my life then, and the sovereign, I forfeited my right to a real human life. The harmony of it from then on was the harmony of the story. Certainly it is a great happiness to be able to turn the things which happen to you into stories. It is perhaps the one perfect happiness that a human being will find in life. But it is at the same time, inexplicably to the uninitiated, a loss, a curse even. What I have gained through these fourteen years is then a knowledge of the story and everything concerning it.'

I have followed the main draft, but there are several others— some only a page or so, others longer—amongst which there are at least five drafts where the stress falls upon the fact that it is Pizzuti who has saved Byron's life. (Even in the main draft, this is still true, although not made entirely clear: if Byron saved Pizzuti's life by paying the ransom, Pizzuti had also done the same for Byron by impersonating him in the first place, and thus saving him from the bandits. The fact that this has not been entirely clarified may be one of the reasons why the story remained unpublished.) Byron and Pizzuti not only physically resembly each other, they are interchangeable: Pizzuti devoted himself to the art of the theatre, Byron to life. Pizzuti, in taking on the role of the artist, had forfeited his right to a real human life.

Pizzuti is not the only one who suffers this fate, however. Byron's life undergoes a similar transformation—after his death. Pizzuti tells him that he has visited him in order to round off his stock of experiences and make it into a unity. '"I am,"' he says, '"going to turn it into a story,"' and adds that Byron's life so far has really amounted to nothing more than a series of minor, self-inflicted defeats:

'And how,' said Lord Byron, 'are you going to make one story of all this?'
'What you need now,' said Pippistrello, 'to round off all these sad

details of fourteen years is one great and deadly defeat, brought on by no fault of your own. That is going to make a unity of the disintegrating elements . . . In a hundred years your works will be read much less than today . . . But one book . . . will be rewritten and re-read, and will each year in a new edition be set upon the shelf.'

'What book is that?' Lord Byron asked.

'Life of Lord Byron,' said Pippistrello.

The end of the story is quite untypical of Isak Dinesen in being much too pat, but the implication is clear enough. In Byron's case also the death of the man is a necessary condition for the existence of art; the real man must die in order that the artist may live.

Isak Dinesen was always bitterly aware of the price she had paid for adopting the life of the artist. In time, as the mask settled more and more firmly into position, she grew used to it and proclaimed the value of all that it represented. But it is worth noting that in this story, written towards the end of her life, she returns to the price that had been exacted. She adopted the mask at the outset of her life as a professional writer to signify a new start and thus fill the vacuum in which she found herself placed; whether it ever completely succeeded in doing so only the face behind it knew.

She lived on at Rungstedlund in constant ill-health, frequently in great pain, several times, during the latter years, at the point of death, but maintaining throughout her indomitable spirit. 'She was,' Thomas Dinesen once said to me, 'simply the bravest person I have ever known,' and he was clearly not thinking solely of her life in Africa, nor only of the way in which she faced disaster there. After long spells in hospital and a series of operations, she was often too ill and weak to sit upright, and was forced to lie flat on the floor, and in that position to dictate her later stories to her secretary. Weighing less than five stone, her face was so wasted and emaciated, her frame so slight and frail, that it seemed miraculous that she could go on living. But her spirited personality was all the more vivid by contrast, and her moral courage, so obvious throughout her whole life, remained undiminished. She had long since chosen the site of her grave in the grounds of Rungstedlund, and visitors were regularly conducted by Miss Svendsen to view it. During one stay in hospital she planned to make a broadcast to tell people how easy it really was to die, but then, as she drily remarked, the point of the broadcast vanished when she again made a recovery. Finally on the 7th September, 1962, at the age of seventy-seven she died in her home; her grave, on a knoll in the park under a large beech tree, is marked by a large stone with only her real name, Karen Blixen, incised upon it. Rungstedlund was donated by her sister, her brothers and herself to be a foundation established for cultural purposes, supported by the royalties from her work. The house itself is now the seat of the Danish Academy, established in 1960 with Isak Dinesen as one of the founder-members, and the grounds of the house, in accordance with her wishes, have been turned into a bird sanctuary, and are open to the public.

A different fate has befallen her farm in Kenya—different, but in some degree peculiarly the same. In the same way that Rungstedlund estate no longer lies out in the open countryside, but survives only in greatly diminished form as a reminder of the past (a fact of which Isak Dinesen herself was always keenly aware), so too with her farm. It is no longer in the untouched country surrounded by the forests and plains of Karen Blixen's day which, together with the Ngong hills at that time 'combined to create a landscape that had not its like in all the world'. Today it forms part of the suburb of Nairobi called 'Karen', and when Kenya celebrated its independence in 1963, the house was bought by the Danish government and presented to the new state to be used as a domestic science centre.

But it is the conditions of isolation Isak Dinesen experienced throughout her later life in Denmark to which we must finally return; these must be stressed, since they also have their part to play in her work. And one can understand the reasons for this sense of isolation. Having grown up in pre-war Denmark, and having passed the happiest and most eventful years of her life in Africa amidst an aristocratic form of society, she returned to the Denmark of the nineteen-thirties—an aristocrat in exile from a world that no longer even existed.

The task of communicating with a public and of establishing some common values and beliefs, within which framework his work can acquire meaning and significance, is difficult for any twentieth-century writer; and this is so even for the writer who lives in his own country and finds his audience there. The task for Isak Dinesen—living in her native country and writing in a foreign language—was doubly difficult. Her public was, quite literally, a divided one—divided between her Danish readers and those in the English-speaking countries (and the diversity covered by that term is significant). Speaking of her readers in the United States in the *Paris Review*, she expressed her great sense of indebtedness to them because *Seven Gothic Tales* was first published there, after she had tried, and failed, to get it accepted by an English publisher. Nevertheless her ties with this readership can hardly be described as close: the first time she actually visited the United States was in 1959, three years before her death. In Denmark the initial reception accorded *Seven Gothic Tales* was a very mixed one: if some critics praised it, there were also others who condemned it as reactionary in spirit, snobbish in its appeal, and decadent, even perverse, in theme. She also felt a deep sense of cleavage between her own work and much of Danish literature during the nineteen-thirties, predominantly realistic in tone and socially engaged. After the war she did in Denmark become the centre of a circle of very much younger writers, intellectuals and artists, but it seems doubtful how much lasting satisfaction and real sense of contact she derived from this. The record of the series of frustrations, then hopes, again followed by fresh disappointment, is set out in full detail in Parmenia Migel's book. As for her ties with England, these were strong, even if rather distant; they were mostly formed through people she had known in Kenya, but most of these died, either before she left the colony, or shortly after.

The point to emphasise, however, is not the relationship—such as it was—to her public within each of these countries. To stress exclusively any one of these relationships is to see her work only from a partial point of view. Something of the full perspective and of its consequences can be inferred from her preface to the Danish version of *Seven Gothic Tales*: it is there that the conditions helping to determine the nature of her work stand out with sharp clarity:

> When I wrote this book for my own pleasure in English, I did not think that it would be of any interest to Danish readers. Now it has had the fate of being translated into other languages, and consequently it has become natural that it should also be published in my own country. Therefore I have wanted it to appear in Denmark as an original Danish edition, and not in any translation however good it might be.[1]

Writing in one language, but always, after *Seven Gothic Tales*, with the intention of translating into her own, it was not only the readership of her books that was divided. So too was their author. Her isolation at the time of writing *Seven Gothic Tales* has already been described; the conditions of her authorship only served to perpetuate this. It is not surprising that she felt distant and aloof from her public—the wonder is that she did not feel even more so. For where essentially was her public? How could she have felt differently under these circumstances? These are the questions which give the measure of her solitariness. It is from this that we can grasp the full significance of the mask she donned, and the conditions dictating her choice of action—if indeed, seen in this way, she had any real choice. Professor Ellmann quotes from an unpublished manuscript of Yeats's mask-play, *The Player Queen*, where a character affirms: 'to be great we must seem so . . . Seeming that goes on for a lifetime is

---

[1] This was her usual procedure, although it is impossible to draw a sharp dividing line between the two languages. Most of her unpublished MSS and drafts of tales are written in English, others, which seem to be predominantly early work, are written in Danish. The working-notes for the stories are generally written in Danish, sometimes they switch between the two languages—occasionally even in mid-sentence.

Nevertheless, she did not make any extravagant claims for her English. In an interview in *Berlingske Tidende* of 10th October, 1958, she was asked which language the stories in *Anecdotes of Destiny* were written in. She replied that they were first written in English (with the exception of 'Tempests') and then translated into Danish; but, she added, 'I don't feel like an English person while I am writing. English people can see immediately that it is a Dane who has written them. English is just easier for me because I lived so many years in Africa.'

no different from reality.'[1] This is also one of Isak Dinesen's most fundamental beliefs; in a way she spent half a lifetime in 'seeming'. She created a personal myth which joined her life and art into a seamless whole, and then embodied this myth in an actual way of life. Instead of seeking to break out of her isolation, she withdrew further into it and emphasised her aloofness by every possible means. She set her stories in the past and thus accentuated their distance from ordinary life in the present. She wrote of the proud solitude of the artist, saw this as his inalienable condition, and all the time she was looking in the mirror of her own art and seeing the reflection of her own solitude. And finally she forfeited her right to a real human life and gained instead a knowledge of the art of the story.

It is at this point we can turn to these stories in more detail and see what this knowledge consisted of.

[1] *Yeats: The Man and The Masks*, p. 176.

PART II

THE ART OF ISAK DINESEN

4

The Function of Imagination

Looking back on Karen Blixen's life from her earliest days at Rungstedlund, throughout the years in Kenya, and then until her death in the same house where she was born, it is possible to discern a kind of pattern in which the different parts of her life fall into place as components of a whole. With its marked symmetry of outline it would seem to have been shaped by circumstances with such an aesthetic eye for the over-all design that her life came to resemble a work of art. So at least Karen Blixen herself saw it. In an interview in *Berlingske Aftenavis*, 24th June, 1950, she regretted the fact that, in her later years, her eyesight had deteriorated. This had been a sad experience, it was true, but it was also one that had had its compensations, for it had meant that somehow things had become more beautiful. She compared this to the way that connoisseurs of art do not stand close to a painting, but take a few steps back so as to appreciate the full effect. 'Perhaps it is just that which the years do with us—or for us! Without any initiative on our part, they lead us back a couple of paces from life and adjust our eyes to get the total impression of what the artist meant.'

These remarks about life offer a precise analogy to what takes place in her stories. There too, by means of the distance maintained between reader and story, we are led back a few paces to get the total impression of what the artist meant by the arrangement of the component parts. Moreover, if Karen Blixen looks at life in the same way as she would view art, this contains a further implication for her work. In her case, unlike so many other writers, it is not only autobiographical experience which, even if very indirectly, provides material for the content of her

73

stories; in addition, the fact that she saw life as a paradigm of art also principally determines their aesthetic form. And the reader, kept at a distance by her narrative form, thus gains the same perspective of her art as she gained of her own life.

In 'The Cardinal's First Tale', after he has narrated his story, the lady in black, who is given no further description than that, tells him that she finds he has now become remote and even rather inhuman. He admits the truth of the charge, but adds:

'You will see the characters of the true story clearly, as if luminous and on a higher plane, and at the same time they may look not quite human, and you may well be a little afraid of them. That is all in the order of things. But I see . . . today, a new art of narration, a novel literature and category of belles-lettres, dawning upon the world . . . And this new art and literature—for the sake of the individual characters in the story, and in order to keep close to them and not to be afraid—will be ready to sacrifice the story itself.

'The individuals of the new books and novels—one by one—are so close to the reader that he will feel a bodily warmth flowing from them, and he will take them to his bosom and make them, in all situations of his life, his companions, friends, and advisers. And while this interchange of sympathy goes on, the story itself loses ground and weight and in the end evaporates. . . . The divine art is the story.'[1]

What the Cardinal is really doing here, of course, is defending his author's conception of the importance of the story itself. The reader's attention (like the writer's) is focused upon the whole; it is not directed to the individual parts—such as the characters. '"I write about characters who together *are* the tale,"' Isak Dinesen said in *Harper's Magazine*. '"I begin, you see, with the flavour of the tale. Then I find the characters, and they take over. They make the design; I simply permit them their liberty . . . I write about characters within a design, how they act upon one another."'[2]

This seems an excellent account of what happens in her stories —except that it is extremely doubtful how far her characters are

[1] *Last Tales*, pp. 23–24.
[2] op. cit., February, 1965, p. 49.

ever really permitted their liberty or allowed to 'take over'. On the contrary, they are kept in very taut leading strings by the author; they neither exist in their own right, nor indeed are they meant to. Isak Dinesen's imagination in the tales does not function primarily in terms of characterisation—one or two major traits are enough and the salient features are established. The characters are assigned to a few clearly defined categories, and the same types are found again and again.

There is also another side to these figures. In most of her stories what the characters say is at least as important as what they do, and this is reflected in the emphasis which is placed upon the dialogue. Some of them are composed almost entirely of this—'Converse at Night in Copenhagen' is precisely what the title indicates; in others, like 'A Consolatory Tale', or 'The Cardinal's First Tale', the story is really told in order to illustrate or develop points in a conversation. In others like 'The Supper at Elsinore' or 'The Deluge at Norderney', the crucial events have actually taken place before the tale starts, and the action consists in bringing the characters together into a place where they can talk. ' "Recount to me your stories,' the Cardinal says in 'The Deluge" ', and this is what they do, in the conversation which lasts throughout the night until day-break. And even in those tales, like 'Copenhagen Season', where the stress falls more on the narration of events, Isak Dinesen places at least one eloquent figure to expound the main themes in the story, as a kind of fixed point around which the whole action revolves.

All of her chief characters then are good talkers—and good listeners. They develop their views at length, expatiate on their subjects, launch into flights of fantasy, illuminate their theme with flashes of wit, while the others listen until their turn comes, or put in a comment, *sotto voce*, which sets off another train of ideas. Sometimes there is a clash of opinion; more often it is a measured exchange of views, even a kind of ordered debate, like the series of ceremonious exchanges which take place between the old lord and his nephew, Adam, in 'Sorrow-Acre'. But the debate is one really held within the mind of their creator rather than one giving the impression of originating from within the characters themselves. It is *her* eloquence which flows directly through them, while they remain immovably fixed in the category to which they have been assigned. What they lose in psychological depth, they gain in rhetorical eloquence; their inner life is externalised, and the movement of their thoughts is expressed through their speech and dialogue. The essence of the relationship between them, in short, consists of a series of verbal exchanges between various interlocutors much more than it is a relationship involving an interaction between fully individualised persons.

The contrast her fictional characters make with the people described in *Out of Africa* has already been noted; but it is possible at this stage to discern an additional reason for this. In the same interview in *Harper's Magazine* she explained why she wrote of characters within a design and of their inter-relationship: 'relations with others is important to me, you see, friendship is precious to me.' It is the reflection of the relationship of the living woman to flesh and blood people which helps impart such humanity and warmth to *Out of Africa*. In that book there *is*—to use the words of the Cardinal to the lady in black—an 'interchange of sympathy', one which is deliberately eschewed in the stories. Why is this excluded? And why is the nature of the relationships in her tales so different from that depicted in *Out of Africa*?

In the tales the focus is shifted from the individual persons to the story as a whole. This adjustment of focus is one defined with such clarity that on one occasion she even represented it in visual terms. The Danish critic, Aage Henriksen, in an essay on Isak Dinesen, says that she would keep her stories by her for years before publishing them, and would lend copies of them to her friends on the strict understanding that they replied to them. Once, a friend of hers, greatly daring, made his reply by writing a sequel; in return, he was given what amounted to a graphic demonstration of the act of the short story:

'What is this supposed to be?' Karen asked. 'It's supposed to be a counter-story,' her friend replied, who had in truth not really considered what it was supposed to be. 'A counter-story, is something which doesn't exist,' she said. 'Nor is there anything called that.' . . . 'I'll show you just what a story looks like,' and she drew a pentagram. 'There! There's nothing to add to this, and nothing to take away. In the same way a story is finished when it is completed.'[1]

It is the figure of the pentagram upon which Isak Dinesen concentrates, and the characters are visualised as being within this. The form of the story, therefore, does not so much develop organically as an interplay between plot and character, but is rather one which is imposed around the characters as a kind of elaborate frame which sets off their actions. A ballet-like achievement of pattern, executed with a stylised grace and a refined decorum is the effect Isak Dinesen often seeks to convey.[2] As a result many of her tales are meant to be enjoyed aesthetically for the clarity and shapeliness of their structure and for the intellectual challenge they offer to unravel their meaning. The individual story is woven together into an intricate arabesque of plot-design; to work out the full consequences of the plot, to interlock all the parts together into an elaborately completed whole is, in fact, the process which engages Isak Dinesen's imagination to its fullest extent. And it is possible to illustrate this process by reference to her manuscripts.

'I begin with the flavour of the tale,' she said. Amongst her manuscripts there are about sixty suggestions and working-notes[3] (all of them quite brief) for the novel, *Albondocani* which she was working on during the last years, but never completed.[4]

---

[1] *Det guddommelige Barn*, p. 98.

[2] Hence also the several references to the art of the ballet in her work. In *Last Tales* the dialogue between the two main characters in 'Converse at Night in Copenhagen', for instance, is described as being a *pas de deux*, and at the climax of their discussion, 'Orosmane's face became clear with an almost luminous pallor. In a last, flying, completely weightless leap—such as in the language of the ballet is called *grand jeté*—he finished off his solo.' (op. cit., p. 339.)

[3] It is difficult to be more precise about the number since it is not always possible to decide whether a note is an idea for a single story, or if several of them would have eventually been combined into one tale.

These notes are all written in Danish and afford an additional illustration of the way she moved between the two languages.

[4] This was to be a very long 'novel' composed of separate units, but all of them inter-related. It is possible to see how her plan would have been carried out in the first section of *Last Tales* entitled 'Chapters from the Novel Albondocani'.

These notes show more precisely what this flavour consisted of, and give a considerable insight into certain aspects of the working of her imagination.

A few of them consist of a concept or an idea around which a story could possibly be constructed; others sketch out a situation or outline a plot:

He who seeks to avoid suffering until he discovers that he can no longer suffer.

The man who is afraid of getting persecution-mania.

On serving man or God. The Cardinal serves man (by entertaining him). The Prince serves God. The Cardinal's reflection.

The mother who complains to the Virgin Mary that she has never seen her child walk. (But the Virgin Mary *has*).

The lover as the hostage of the deceived husband.

The man who heard the bird singing and fifty years went by.

The bull-fighter who trained the bull in order to revenge himself upon his rival.

The inquisitor who removes the heretic from the stake to learn how it feels to be burned.

The man who begins something in earnest, which the others, in jest, have made him start in order to make a fool of him, and who sets about it so earnestly that the others have to let him go on.

The swindler who passes a false pearl off as a genuine one, but the prince has put a genuine pearl in its place. (Or the swindler has replaced the genuine pearl with a false one, and the prince changes them again.) At any rate a triumph for virtue. Cf. the passage in Aladdin where Morgiane brings the sultan jewels which she herself believes to be made of glass.

The condemned man's friend who obtains his pardon by putting all the clocks back. The evil judge believes that the clocks are right, but thinks that the man who applies for a pardon is mistaken, and that the execution is to take place one hour later than is actually the case. Therefore he agrees to pardon the condemned man when the clock strikes two.

The old gentleman who was fortunate enough to live in Seville thirty years after Don Juan had seduced the women there. The unhappy girl who was not seduced by Don Juan.

There are also some other ideas which are more in the nature of aphorisms; for example:

Praying to God and tossing for heads or tails (vice versa).

Living for others leads to materialism since others can only be helped materially.

All despair stems from moral indignation. If old age were caused by the interference of another person it would be insufferable. A comparison of man's attitude to God with that of the citizen's attitude to the authorities.

Having got the initial idea or sketch of a situation, the next stage was the one which took Isak Dinesen most time. Keeping the drafts by her for years so that she had several different stories on the stocks at the same time, she would recast them again and again. The painstaking care with which she elaborated her plots is amply demonstrated by her manuscripts. She would take a particular incident in a story, amplify it in one draft, then becoming dissatisfied, would abandon it. Then she would start another version of the same incident, this time condense it, and try to fit it into another place in the story, until this too would be given up. Beginning all over again, she would rewrite the whole tale, re-arranging the sequence of the action, cutting here, transposing there, omitting some parts altogether, adding a detail here, altering a character's actions there. It is practically impossible to trace the chronological order in which the different drafts were written, and this is a direct consequence of the way in which she worked, weaving back and forth, constantly re-arranging her material and shuffling the different parts around until they were finally composed into the order which satisfied her exacting demands. More evidence of the care to which even the smallest details were subjected is given in a reply which she made to some criticisms of 'The Roads round Pisa' by the Danish scholar Hans Brix. Through a very detailed analysis of this tale Brix had tried to show certain inconsistencies in the plot. Isak Dinesen, however, turned the tables by refuting these objections in an even more minutely detailed analysis, showing the way in which it was constructed so that everything was interlinked to form an indivisible whole.

These manuscripts take us into her workroom and show us something of her method and the processes which the stories underwent during their composition, but it is also possible to discern the fundamental idea controlling these processes in her published work. In *Out of Africa* she describes a game she had been taught as a child; as an illustration of her method and intention it could hardly be improved upon:

> When I was a child I was shown a picture,—a kind of moving picture inasmuch as it was created before your eyes and while the artist was telling the story of it. This story was told, every time, in the same words.
>
> In a little round house with a round window and a little triangular garden in front there lived a man.[1]

This house and garden are drawn on a sheet of paper. One night the man hears a terrible noise, rushes out, runs first one way then the other, and each time he does this, his movements are drawn on the paper. He stumbles over a big stone, falls into ditches, finds the water rushing out of a dam, and then has much trouble in plugging it. Finally he returns, utterly weary, to the house, and goes to bed. The next morning he looks out of the window and sees what it has all added up to—the picture of a stork. She adds this comment:

> I am glad that I have been told this story and I will remember it in the hour of need. The man in the story was cruelly deceived, and had obstacles put in his way. He must have thought: 'What ups and downs! What a run of bad luck!' He must have wondered what was the idea of all his trials, he could not know that it was a stork. But through them all he kept his purpose in view, nothing made him turn round and go home, he finished his course, he kept his faith. That man had his reward. In the morning he saw the stork. He must have laughed out loud then.
>
> The tight place, the dark pit in which I am now lying, of what bird is it the talon? *When the design of my life is completed, shall I, shall other people see a stork?*[2]

[1] *Out of Africa*, pp. 251 ff.
[2] My emphasis.

The characters in Isak Dinesen's stories can also be deceived and have obstacles put in their way, but when the design of their life has been completed, the meaning is made plain—at the end of the story. Standing back and seeing the whole in retrospect, like the man looking back on the events of the previous night, the idea becomes clear—both to them and to the reader.

Isak Dinesen's major intention of showing the completed design, to which nothing can be added and from which nothing can be subtracted, gives one of the principle reasons for the fact that her tales are set in the past. As we have noted, the past is the dimension in which she felt her imagination could range most freely, and when asked on one occasion if all her tales were set in the nineteenth century, she indicated another of the reasons for this in her reply: 'I may begin in the eighteenth century and come right up to the First World War; my calendar is flexible. Those times have been sorted out; they are clearly visible.' And she goes on with words that directly recall her statement of what she believed took place in life as a result of the passing of time: 'The present is always unsettled, no one has time to contemplate it in tranquillity. No painter wants the subject right under his nose; one wants to stand back and study . . . with half-closed eyes.'[1]

The fact that the setting in the past causes a distillation of the major issues and liberates the imagination is nowhere in Isak Dinesen's work better illustrated than in 'Sorrow-Acre', one of the finest of all her tales. It is based on a folk-tale from the south of Jutland;[2] the details vary, but the most important version for our purpose is given in F. Ohrt's *Udvalgte Sønderjydske Folkesagn* (*Selected Folk-Tales from South Jutland*), published in 1919. This version runs as follows:

During a flood with high tidal waves, a good deal of flotsam drifted ashore near Ballum. Amongst it, a young man from the town recognised some pieces belonging to his family, and started salvaging them. Whilst he was doing this, one of the robbers from

[1] *Harper's Magazine*, February, 1965, p. 49.
[2] The legend was also used for the modern Danish opera, *Høst* (*Harvest*), by Svend S. Schultz, first performed in 1950.

Skærbæk came and wanted some of it. They started fighting, and the young lad unfortunately killed his opponent. At that time, however, these beach-robbers were so powerful that they had him condemned to death at the court-house. His mother, deeply distressed by this, went to the Count at his castle of Skakkenborg, told him of her grief, and implored him to show mercy towards her son. The Count promised her to do so on the condition that she must mow a field of barley between sunrise and sunset. This field was so large that four men would have much labour to cut it in one day. If she could do it, her son would be set free. The mother accepted the task, and did finish it. When she had cut the last handful with her sickle, she said,

Now the sun will set
Now God's mercy I will get.

But at the very moment when she raised herself from her bent position, her back broke and she fell dead. The mother was buried in the churchyard at Ballum. On her grave, a stone has been laid, on which she is drawn with a sheaf and sickle in her arm. The field where she cut the corn is still shown. To this day it is known as Sorrow-Acre.[1]

The date of the events giving rise to the folk-tale can be determined quite accurately since the flood took place in 1634.

In March, 1931, the Danish writer Paul la Cour published a much longer version of the folk-tale in the periodical *Tilskueren*. The original version as found in Ohrt's collection was also included. But although this contribution to *Tilskueren* was almost certainly the source of Isak Dinesen's short story, it differs considerably both from la Cour's version and from the original folk-tale itself.

Paul la Cour followed the details of the original tale very closely, but considering these bare details as being 'schematic and too condensed', he lengthened them very considerably, mainly by dwelling on the feelings of the mother, through whom much of the story is presented. The whole focus is consequently shifted on to her, and the final result is one in which the feelings receive as much emphasis as the narration of the events. Isak

[1] It may be of interest to add that these details are quite true. Even today, if one visits the village of Ballum on the west coast of Jutland, one can find what is said to be Anne-Marie's grave in the churchyard with the sheaf and the sickle carved on the stone and see the field still named 'Sorrow-Acre'.

Dinesen's short story, however, offers a sharp contrast with la Cour's, since the stress falls upon the story itself, while the details of the narrative, as found in the folk-tale, are extensively changed.

In 'Sorrow-Acre', a young man on the estate of a Danish nobleman has been accused of setting fire to one of the barns. Anne-Marie, his widowed mother, intercedes for him, and, like the mother in the folk-tale, is told that if she can cut a field of corn between sunrise and sunset her son will be set free. But if she fails, the case against her son will go through, and she will never see him again. To this agreement the lord pledges his word and Anne-Marie accepts the conditions. We learn of this in retrospect, since the story begins with the thoughts and reminiscences of the lord's young nephew, Adam, newly returned from a long stay in England. It is through his eyes that we see much of the action, and the conflict of principles forming the core of the story emerges from the conversations which take place between the two men when Adam entreats the lord to retract his word, and thereby rescind the agreement with Anne-Marie. The lord steadfastly refuses to do this, and the rest of the story follows the folk-tale with the mother dying just as she has completed her task. The son is freed, and the field afterwards is named Sorrow-Acre.

From this some of the changes made will be apparent; two, in particular, are very significant. A completely new character, Adam, is introduced, and moreover his importance in the story is even stressed by the method of narration. The other major change is that the date at which the events take place has been altered. It is still kept in the past, but the times have been moved forward by well over a hundred years. This date is just as firmly given as in the folk-tale, though more indirectly. During the course of the story, Adam lends his uncle a book which has recently been published; it is described as a tragedy dealing with the gods of Nordic mythology, by Johannes Ewald (the same poet who had lived for a time at Rungstedlund), and it is clear the work is *Balders Død* (*The Death of Balder*), first published in 1775. The introduction of a new main character and a shift time from 1634 to about 1775—why are these changes made?

These two alterations are connected and together point to one of the major themes. The story is now set in the period when the long-established, semi-feudal, landed society of the eighteenth century (reminiscent of that in Kenya) is beginning to face the challenge of new ideas. And in this challenge, the ethos of the age in decline is more sharply defined and is made, in Isak Dinesen's own phrase about the winnowing effect of the past, 'clearly visible'. Moreover, the fact that it is *Balders Død* which gives rise to the discussions between Adam and his uncle is clearly intended not only to give the period in which 'Sorrow-Acre' is set, but also to throw the clash between the opposing attitudes into even sharper relief. Ewald's drama centres on Balder, who in this work is a Nordic demi-god driven to his death by the force of his irresistible passion for Nanna, a mortal woman; although a demi-god, he is powerless to control his emotions. For the old lord the main significance of the book is that it marks the emergence of a new era, which 'has made to itself a God in its own image, an emotional God', and is thus in complete opposition to the ideal of responsibility and omnipotence upon which he bases his conduct, and which is represented for him by the ancient gods of classical mythology. In other words, the setting of the folk-tale has been transferred so that Isak Dinesen's short story now stands at the cross-roads of one of the great movements in European social and cultural history; and the figure of Adam is introduced to be the voice of the new age. The two ways of life confront each other in his impassioned plea to the lord:

'In this very place where we now stand,' said the old Lord, then, with hauteur, 'I gave Anne-Marie my word.' 'My Uncle!' said Adam. 'A life is a greater thing even than a word. Recall that word, I beseech you, which was given in caprice, as a whim.' . . . 'You will have learnt in school,' said his Uncle, 'that in the beginning was the word. It may have been pronounced in caprice, as a whim, the Scripture tells us nothing about it. It is still the principle of our world, its law of gravitation. My own humble word has been the principle of the land on which we stand, for an age of man.' . . . 'You are mistaken!' cried Adam, 'the word is creative, it is imagination, daring and passion . . . And when you look at the people, simpler than we, and nearer to the heart of nature, who do not analyse their feelings, whose life is one with the life of the earth, do they not inspire in you tenderness, respect, reverence even? This woman is ready to die for her son,—will it ever happen to you or me that a woman willingly gives up her life for us?'[1]

A ready sympathy is aroused by the views expressed here by Adam. But perhaps the sympathy is felt a little too readily and the identification with one character made too swiftly. For part of the greatness of 'Sorrow-Acre' lies in the fact that the reader is gradually forced away from this incipient identification with one character, is made to stand at a distance, and thus gain a clearer insight and imaginative understanding of the old lord's role, and everything which this represents. In particular we are made to realise the full implications of what is merely a 'caprice' or 'whim' for Adam. The conflicting issues in 'Sorrow-Acre' are not simply formulated in abstract terms in the discussions; they take on a life of their own which is rendered by the complete story. They are really threads woven into the finished pattern, and which must be related to the whole; indeed the reader is compelled to do this by the narrative method.

The artistry, by which the reader is made to look at the old lord's role with an imaginative perception and a gradually quickened understanding, needs to be stressed. The method of narration is actually used by Isak Dinesen to weight the scales against the lord, since we see him mainly through the eyes of a highly critical Adam. It is a criticism presented with scrupulous honesty and to which full weight is given. And although Anne-Marie dies at the supreme moment of her love and glory, having kept faith and finally conquered over all her tribulation like the man in the story of the stork, nevertheless, her sacrifice, exacted by the conditions imposed by the lord, is not minimised in any way. On the contrary, it has been counted, and counted against him, in the finely rendered description of her death at the end. But the old lord is neither individualised, nor given any very human quality; he appears in the story as remote and as inhuman as the Cardinal seemed to the lady in black. Like her, he is not even given a name, but remains from first to last simply 'the old lord'. He is in fact, the product of a completely

[1] *Winter's Tales,* pp. 58–59.

disciplined imagination, imperturbably keeping its distance, holding its powers rigorously within bounds, dispassionately subduing to the total demands of the story any innate sympathy for a particular character, or any trace of nostalgia for a lost order of society.

Although the short story has a much more limited compass than the novel, it still remains clear that Isak Dinesen's imagination, when engaged in representing a past age, does not belong to that type—like Thackeray's, for instance, in *Henry Esmond*—which musters a wealth of historical detail into a composite picture, and reconstructs the life of a period in that way. Instead she fastens on the more general features of a past era and etches these in, sharply, but economically. The figure of the old lord is an example of this, for his lack of individualisation in the story is partly a reflection of his social position in that age. Thus he becomes a typical representative of the *ancien régime*, of its way of life and ideals. Describing the life of the great manor-houses, the narrator remarks:

> To the King and the country, to his family and to the individual Lord of the manor himself it was a matter of minor consequence which particular Rosenkrantz, Juel or Skeel, out of a long row of Fathers and Sons, at the moment in his person incarnated the fields and woods, the peasants, cattle and game of the estate.[1]

The reader's imaginative understanding of the old lord's character also extends to the part he plays. His character in the story is his part in life; the two cannot be separated, for they are made into one by the way in which he is presented. By her way of depicting him, Isak Dinesen succeeds, against all modern predilections, and against all odds, in investing his duties with a certain nobility and grandeur and in compelling our respect. He is seen as the embodiment of the duties of the great land-owners of the past both to their land and to the people living on it, as an incarnation of the principle of *noblesse oblige*. This, in turn, shows the part which the fine evocation of the Danish landscape at the beginning contributes to the whole. Here Isak Dinesen really does 'stand back and study a landscape with half-closed

[1] *Winter's Tales*, pp. 31–32.

eyes'; but the details, painted in so deftly, are not there merely to provide local colour. Like the splendour of the descriptions in *Out of Africa*, which affords a fitting background to the heroic nature of life there, these details in 'Sorrow-Acre' are also made to contribute to the total effect. The description is of a landscape —but of a landscape with figures; rendered in terms of the people who inhabit it, it ceases to be merely this, and becomes a land where life falls into an ordered pattern of existence, drawn by generations of people, traced by stability, marked by tradition and order, and maintained throughout the centuries by these same qualities:

> A child of the country would read this open landscape like a book. The irregular mosaic of meadows and cornlands was a picture, in timid green and yellow, of the people's struggle for its daily bread, —the centuries had taught it to plough and sow in this way . . . But where, amongst cupolar woods and groves the lordly, pyramidal silhouette of the cut lime-avenues rose in the air, there a big country-house lay . . . as firmly rooted in the soil of Denmark as the peasants' huts.[1]

In this rendering of a way of life, country-house and peasant hut, peasant and lord, are inter-dependent parts. 'Sorrow-Acre' itself is but one field, a single piece in the mosaic of the Danish countryside. Much more is at stake for the lord than Anne-Marie's individual fate and destiny—or even his own. Representation of the unity of this life becomes the design of the story —design in every sense—which is reaffirmed at the close, when, in the evening-light, the people left in the field after Anne-Marie's death bind up the corn she has cut: 'the old lord stayed with them for a long time, stepping along a little, and again standing still. As it grew darker he could walk up quite close to them or move amongst them, without being recognised.'[2]

The old order has been re-affirmed and the unity of this life endures—but for how long? As in Kenya, after Berkeley Cole's death, history itself and historical change break into this stable world, set in the past and enclosed within the framework of the

[1] *Winter's Tales*, pp. 30–31.
[2] ibid., p. 69.

story: Adam has his destiny to fulfil. His relationship to the lord's young wife is not elaborated, but the suggestion of their growing intimacy also forms part of the story. There is no heir to the land, and it has been foretold Adam that a son of his will inherit the estate. The setting in the past, which causes the conflict between the two ways of life, also indicates the way the issues will be decided. And it is one which heightens the old lord's stature into that of an indomitable figure defending a dying order.

One final point remains to be made about the lord, for concealed behind him can be discerned much of Isak Dinesen's own attitude. For him 'tragedy is the privilege of man, his highest privilege', whereas 'the true art of the Gods is the comic'. He develops this belief by saying that on earth, the aristocrats 'who stand in lieu of the Gods . . . should leave to our vassals their monopoly of tragedy, and for ourselves accept the comic with grace',[1] and he acts accordingly by leaving to Anne-Marie her monopoly of tragedy. But if she is made into a tragic figure by the lord's actions, he is made into something very different by the author. By implying that the old lord will be made a cuckold by his young wife and Adam, Isak Dinesen has thus identified him with one of the most traditional figures of comedy. And in this lies the paradox. For by doing this, she has implicitly endorsed the validity of his attitude and beliefs, solely by means of the story itself and the turn it is given, not by any overt expression of sympathy with his ideals. The lord says that 'the very same fatality which, in striking the burgher or peasant will become tragedy, with the aristocrat is exalted to the comic. By the grace and wit of our acceptance hereof our aristocracy is known'. If these beliefs govern his behaviour in 'Sorrow-Acre', they also define with equal force that of Karen Blixen herself as revealed in *Out of Africa*. The story's historical setting is eighteenth-century Denmark, but personal remembrance of grace and wit also constitutes a part of the imagination which created 'Sorrow-Acre'.

Some further qualities of Isak Dinesen's imagination, deriving from the fact that the stories are set in the past, can be explored

[1] *Winter's Tales*, pp. 52–53.

by a comparison of the tale, 'Copenhagen Season', with an unpublished one, 'Carnival'. 'Carnival' is set in the mid-nineteen-twenties, and thus is exceptional in that it falls quite outside the period in which she usually places her tales. In it a supper-party is held in a large house on the outskirts of Copenhagen after a masked ball in the town. The guests come to the house in the fancy-dress they have worn at the ball; they are all depicted as bright young things of the period, and give, what is to us now, a rather faded air of determined frivolity. There is one character who is an exception to this: an elderly painter called Rosendahl, who is described thus:

> Since it seemed strange that such a very brilliant person should have a little full-moon face, with no features, hair or expression to speak of, indeed most of all like the posterior of a baby, the pupils of his painting school, who loved him, had developed a theory that there had been a shifting about in his anatomy, and that he had an eminently radiant and expressive face at the other place.

This is transferred almost verbatim to 'Copenhagen Season', where it is used to describe the artist, Professor Sivertsen. But this is not the only similarity between the two stories.

In the conversation during supper, Rosendahl states that, in his belief, the present age is inferior to previous times because it has banished tragedy from life; the way in which this has been done, however, is never made very clear, for he does not see this in social terms, but instead illustrates this absence of tragedy aesthetically, in terms of painting. Black, he says, is necessary for a painting since it gives a contrast to all the other colours; if the painter is denied its use, all the other hues pale into insignificance. Similarly tragedy is an essential part of life, and it is really one of man's rights to be allowed to preserve a sense of the darker side of life. Talking of the slum-clearance recently undertaken in Copenhagen, he says: 'We had much trouble in making some of the old inhabitants move away,—good, decent people, who clung to the right of man, to preserve a little bit of darkness of their own.'

The remainder of the story can be quickly summarised. All the people present are well-off, and they decide to draw lots to

see which one of them shall live on their pooled income for a
year, during which time the others are to be penniless. A man
enters at this point, dressed all in black as Zamor, Madame du
Barry's Negro page. At the sight of him the painter thinks:
'These people see in him only a Carnival joke. But there is more
here. Perhaps a good deal of suffering, despair, a surprise to
the whole party.' A surprise it is. Holding up the party with
a gun, he demands their money, saying that he is a desperate
man and not to be trifled with since he has already killed one
person, the woman who owned the antique shop where he
worked. They treat this fairly calmly, and instead persuade him
to take part in their lottery. One of the characters wins, and
announces that she will take Zamor with her for the year 'to be
my conscience. Shall I not be allowed to have a conscience,
Rosie? Something black in my life, a little *mouche* on my
soul?'

The plot has been rather baldly summarised because one can
thus see the significance of the striking contrast this story, taking
place in the twentieth century, makes with the rest of Isak
Dinesen's work, set a hundred to a hundred and fifty years ago.
The highly melodramatic nature of the plot is very apparent, and
this is even heightened by the incongruity this makes with such
features of twentieth-century life as slum-clearance and with the
modernity of the characters—most of them have sports-cars, one
of them has his own aeroplane. In 'Carnival' the representation
of an historical period has really dwindled to a passing reference
to an antique shop. Nevertheless, although the plot is melodramatic, it is no more so than most of Isak Dinesen's other
tales; there is little to choose between the plot of this story and,
say, that of 'The Deluge at Norderney', where a valet murders
his master, the Cardinal, in order to impersonate him; or that
of 'The Supper at Elsinore' in which the ghost of a pirate returns
to Elsinore to visit his two sisters. In these stories, however, the
melodrama, instead of being incongruously at odds with the
contemporary scene, becomes simply one more aspect marking
the story off from our own day and age. It is not only the
author's imagination that is liberated by setting the stories in the
past, so too is the reader's.

If the way in which the modern age has banished tragedy from life is never made clear in 'Carnival', in 'Copenhagen Season' this becomes a major theme. And the person who expresses it is Professor Sivertsen. 'What is it?' he asks, thinking aloud,

> 'that is an absurd and preposterous thing, a ridiculous thing to carry about with you in life, and which is at the same time the rare spice by the aid of which tragedy is created? . . . It is named honour . . . the idea of honour.
> 'All tragedies . . . from *Phaedra* and *Antigone* to *Kabale und Liebe* and *Hernani* . . . are determined by the idea of honour. The idea of honour does not save humanity from suffering, but it enables it to write a tragedy. An age which can prove the wounds of the hero on the battlefield to be equally painful whether in the breast or in the back, may produce great scientists and statisticians. But a tragedy it cannot write.
> 'Those very pleasant people, your grandchildren,' he went on, 'at their tea-party in a hundred years will have their troubles, but they will have no tragedy. They will have debts—troublesome things—but no debt of honour.'[1]

The story is set in Denmark in the eighteen-seventies and its remoteness from the present is stressed. It is a period for Isak Dinesen hall-marked by a code of honour, and it is just as obvious from this story, as it was from 'Sorrow-Acre', that an age which held honour so dearly is one which Isak Dinesen's imagination found much more congenial than modern times. Ib Angel, based as we have seen upon her father, has fought a duel of honour, even though duels have been prohibited. The age is also one nearing its end and standing on the threshold of the present. But before it finally passes away, it gives Ib, the epitome of the period, the opportunity to perform a tragic action by steadfastly maintaining its code.

Ib Angel is in love with Adelaide, who belongs to one of the noblest families in the Danish aristocracy. They own vast estates, and the way in which Isak Dinesen's imagination is stirred by the life they represent is very apparent in the following passage:

[1] *Last Tales*, pp. 275–276.

Such vast areas of land spread before it to all sides that the domain had become a kingdom of its own: tall forests with deer and fallow-deer in them, fields and meadows with clear streams winding through them, lakes and ponds gazing sleepily up into the sky. Seven hundred copyhold farms lay on the lea-side of woods and ridges of the estate, forty-two good Lutheran churches kept a pious watch on its hills. Above the tall trees of the park the copper-roofed towers of the castle caught the golden rays of the rising and the setting sun. The centuries had soldered land and name into a unity, so that today no one could tell whether the land belonged to the name or the name to the land. Mill-wheels turned in the rivers for the name, ploughs broke its deep soil for it behind patient, shaggy horses.[1]

The social position of Adelaide's family plays an essential part in the tale. Ib Angel does not belong to the aristocracy, and the barrier this establishes entirely precludes any question of marriage between them. In what is to be their last meeting, which takes place in secret, it is made clear that if he personifies the honour of his age, Adelaide is also representative of it in another way. Without realising the implication of her suggestion, she tells him that she is willing to go on meeting him illicitly:

> For a second her total and absolute ignorance of the coarser facts of life, which was the *fine fleur* of her education and upbringing—as of the education and upbringing of all noble young girls of her age—and had been obtained with such a tenacity of purpose and such continuous watchfulness as later ages cannot imagine or believe, awakened in him the reverence which was the highest product of the education of all noble young men . . . He knew well enough what, according to the code of orthodox morality he ought to say to her . . . But orthodox morality had become a thing of the vanished past . . . Here at last were Ib and Adelaide, alone in the universe . . . And then, just then, at the moment when he had quashed all outside laws, the law of his own being spoke out and passed sentence on him.[2]

Ib sacrifices his love to his code of honour and thus fulfils the conditions which Professor Sivertsen had stated as being necessary for tragedy.

[1] *Last Tales*, pp. 254–255.
[2] ibid., pp. 303–304.

In 'Carnival', the past with its idea of tragedy offers a contrast to the present, but it is one only stated, and remains a shadow without substance. The situation is exactly reversed in 'Copenhagen Season'; there, a past era is concretely described, takes on form and substance, and by means of this the present time is weighed in the balance and found wanting. Like Professor Sivertsen, who condemns the times to come because, lacking honour, they lack also the conditions necessary to create a tragedy, Isak Dinesen's moral condemnation of the present and approbation of a past ethos are also expressed in aesthetic terms and implicitly testified to by the very existence of the story itself.

So far we have been considering the way in which Isak Dinesen's imagination functions particularly in its concern with the past, but there is also a way in which it is engaged with the present, namely, in the person of the reader of her tales. 'It is not a bad thing in a tale that you understand only half of it,' Lincoln Forsner says in 'The Dreamers',[1] before embarking upon his story; it is a remark that represents another facet of Isak Dinesen's attitude to the reader, and the story of 'The Young Man with the Carnation' helps define this more closely.

The main character, Charlie Despard, is a writer who believes that his creative imagination has now atrophied so that he will never be able to write another book. He feels that he has been turned from 'a human being into printed matter', and that of his own free will, but without, until then, counting the cost, he has exchanged all the things that constitute life for 'the words that describe them'. Arriving late at night in Antwerp to rejoin his wife, he goes up to her hotel room and gets into bed without waking her. Shortly after, he hears someone try the door, opens it, and finds a young man with a carnation in his button-hole standing outside. The man apologises when he sees Charlie, and leaves. But Charlie is unable to sleep and begins to speculate about the young man, for, in his thoughts, he has come to represent everything in life he himself has renounced in order to become an artist:

[1] *Seven Gothic Tales*, p. 279.

For here, he knew, was the glory, the meaning and the key of life.
The young man with the carnation had got it. . . . Once upon a
time, it seemed to him, he too had known it, and had let go his
hold, and here he was, forever doomed. Oh God, God in Heaven,
at what time had his own road taken off from the road of the young
man with the carnation?[1]

He gets up and goes down to the harbour where he spends the
rest of the night in an inn talking to some sailors; during the
time he is there, he feels his imagination again stirring to life and
tells them a story.[2]

In the morning Charlie returns to the hotel, meets his wife,
then discovers that the room he had entered the previous evening was in fact not hers. His imagination now even more aroused
by the mystery in which he has inadvertently been involved, he
decides that he will write a story about it:

> As Charlie now looked back on the happenings of the night, with
> the experienced eye of an author of fiction, they moved him as
> mightily as if they had been out of a book of his own. He drew in
> his breath deeply. 'Almighty God,' he said from the bottom of his
> heart, 'as the heavens are higher than the earth, so are Thy short
> stories higher than our short stories.' He went through all the
> details slowly, and surely, as a mathematician sets up and solves an
> equation.[3]

A rather obtrusive colloquy follows between God and Charlie,
in which God maintains that to be isolated from life is an irrevocable edict imposed on the artist; through this dialogue Charlie
Despard becomes reconciled to his lot and sees life as providing
the raw material for the artist's creative imagination and human
existence being of importance because it affords a subject for
aesthetic activity. The tale ends with his thoughts returning to

[1] *Winter's Tales*, p. 10.

[2] Lady Helena of this inset story appears in one draft of an unpublished
tale called 'Anna', in which she comes to Italy on the same quest for a particular shade of blue. The story of her life does not form an integral part of
the action of that main tale either. She leaves her money when she dies to
Anna, a peasant girl whom she has met on her travels, and Anna is the main
character.

Judging from a list of contents amongst Isak Dinesen's MSS, 'Anna' at
one time was intended to form part of *Anecdotes of Destiny*.

[3] *Winter's Tales*, p. 25.

the young man and the story he is now certain he will write about him.

His solution to the equation posed by the young man is that he has witnessed a romantic assignation between two lovers, and it is this assignation he will write his story about; but it is by no means certain that this interpretation is the only construction which can be placed on the events since other possibilities easily suggest themselves to the reader. And the fact that the options are left open is something deliberately intended by Isak Dinesen. 'The Young Man with the Carnation' is really a kind of palimpsest; one interpretative design has been drawn and made complete, but beneath this pattern, other outlines can be discerned. The tale not only describes the way in which the artist's creative faculties are aroused; the reader's imagination is also awakened by following the events and attempting to square them with his own interpretation.

At the same time the story has certain radical flaws. The description of Charlie Despard going through the details of the plot like a mathematician setting up, and then solving, an equation, reveals a disturbingly high degree of contrived ingenuity, and the plot itself is more like the preliminary sketches for a story one finds among Isak Dinesen's manuscripts than a tale that has gradually been enriched over a long period of time by her usual vein of fantasy. And the similarity with these working-sketches is really no coincidence, since the story is actually meant to illustrate the role allotted the reader within her scheme of artistry as a whole. Further evidence of this—and one which exposes even more clearly the weaknesses of this story—is provided by 'The Caryatides'.

Although it appears in *Last Tales*, 'The Caryatides' was actually written many years previously; like 'Carnival' it was originally intended as part of *Seven Gothic Tales*, but was subsequently dropped from that collection.[1] First published

[1] The following table of contents for *Seven Gothic Tales* (at that time given the title, *The Poet and other Tales*) can be found among the MSS: 'The Roads round Pisa', 'Carnival', 'The Monkey', 'The Old Chevalier', 'The Deluge at Norderney', 'The Dreamers', 'The Caryatides', and 'The Poet'. Thus both 'Carnival' and 'The Caryatides' were dropped from the published volume, and 'The Supper at Elsinore' substituted instead.

in Danish in 1938 as an unfinished tale by the Swedish literary periodical, *Bonniers Litterära Magasin*, it was still incomplete when included some twenty years later in *Last Tales*. When it first appeared, the editor of the periodical, in a short introduction, suggested that this unfinished state was really an intentional effect:

A fragment often has a more suggestive quality than a finished work of art . . . Nor am I quite convinced that the sphinx-like author has not deliberately left the story unfinished, just because she has given us the key—the secret code of the combination to the way it continues. In reply to an enquiry she said, 'It is best that the story finishes where it does—best for the characters and best for us. I did not dare go on.'[1]

There really seems no doubt that the story is deliberately left unfinished. The length of time between writing and first publishing it (at least four years, since *Seven Gothic Tales* came out in 1934), and then all the years that elapsed before it was finally included in *Last Tales*, point very strongly to this. But the most convincing reason lies in the fact that without a shadow of a doubt it *is* best that it finishes where it does and the riddle remains unsolved. It is better that the reader's imagination should be stimulated to try and unravel the Gordian knot than that the sphinx-like author should go on to cut it; nor is it surprising that she did not dare go on—and run the risk of an anti-climax.

The problem in 'The Caryatides' is a much more integral part of the plot than in 'The Young Man', and there is a highly imaginative aura cast around all the events by a gypsy, who has the reputation of being a witch, and plays a key-role in the action. Moreover, whereas Charlie Despard was an artist with no roots anywhere, here the characters are firmly placed in a particular context, and again it is one which defines the role they play in the story—particularly that of the women, as Caryatides, who uphold a semi-feudal world by the position they occupy in it. Philippe is married to a woman, who, he discovers after their marriage, is really his sister. If the true nature of their

[1] *Bonniers Litterära Magasin*, March, 1938, pp. 163–164.

relationship is revealed, it will bring the world of their estate, together with the lives of all those dependent upon them, down in ruins. The story breaks off before Philippe's wife discovers the truth, but she may—or may not—be about to do so.

'The Caryatides' is really a virtuoso exercise in pure ambivalence; the reader is mischievously teased into participation in the game—and most of his enjoyment of the story must stem from this fact being recognised. The sphinx is really wearing a smile. 'It is not a bad thing in a tale that you understand only half of it'; it is more, it is an essential condition of Isak Dinesen's art.

In his essay, 'Notes on the Novel' Ortega y Gasset writes that, if we examine the way in which the novel has developed from its beginnings to the present day, we can observe that, from being narrative and indirect, the novel has become direct and descriptive, or, what he calls, 'presentative'. It is a generalisation that would require some considerable qualification when applied to the novel's development as a whole, but its interest lies in the way Ortega defines 'presentative':

> .... when we are fascinated by a novel it is not because of its subject, not because we are curious to know what happened to Mr So-and-so. The subject of any novel can be told in a few words and in this form holds no interest. A summary narration is not to our taste; we want the novelist to linger and to grant us good long looks at his personages, their being, and their environment till we have had our fill and feel that they are close friends whom we know thoroughly in all the wealth of their lives. That is what makes of the novel an essentially slow-moving genre as either Goethe or Novalis observed. I will go even further and say that today the novel is, and must be, a sluggish form—the very opposite therefore of a story.[1]

As a description of what Isak Dinesen does *not* do this could hardly be improved upon. She neither lingers in this way, nor gives us good long looks at her personages, nor do we ever become close friends. On the other hand, 'summary narration' could hardly be bettered as a description of her technique: her method is that which Ortega criticises sharply when employed by the novelist:

[1] *The Dehumanization of Art and Other Writings on Art and Culture*, New York, 1956, p. 61.

We want to see the life of the figures in a novel, not to be told it. Any reference, allusion, narration only emphasizes the absence of what it alludes to. . . . When I read in a novel 'John was peevish' it is as though the writer invited me to visualize, on the strength of his definition, John's peevishness in my own imagination. That is to say, he expects me to be the novelist.[1]

This is precisely an account of what happens with Isak Dinesen. We, too, as we have noted, are always kept aware of what is absent in her tales: given a summary, we are expected to amplify it until the full meaning is grasped. In fact the principle of omission operates just as stringently in her stories at it did in *Out of Africa*, and becomes a basic part of her artistic design; for it is a design in which the reader's imagination is compelled to participate in the very act of creation.

Her tales frequently seem baffling whilst reading them—and they are made deliberately so by the author. Time and again motives for the characters' actions are concealed, links in the plot are obscured, the significance of incidents is veiled at the time they happen, and their meaning is only elucidated later. This does not constitute wilful mystification for its own sake. The characters do trace out a meaningful design, but they are not fully aware of its import until the end—nor is the reader. If they are left in the dark, he too is given very little light. In retrospect, however, everything is clarified, but like the characters, the reader has to work at this. Assigned a part to play, he is made to play it by her conception of the artist's function: Isak Dinesen calls the tune and it demands an attentive listener. And all this is done in accordance with a definite creed that an atmosphere of mystery and a state of half-knowledge is the indispensable condition for calling the imagination into play—in life as well as in art.

The fundamental question this raises then is why does Isak Dinesen place such a high value on the role of the imagination? What, in the last analysis, is her conception of the artist's function and of his relationship to the reader? A description of this relationship is given in 'A Consolatory Tale', the other story in

[1] *The Dehumanization of Art*, pp. 58–59.

Winter's Tales in which Charlie Despard appears. Quoting the injunction to love thy God, he changes it somewhat. '"Thou shalt," he says, '"love they art with all thy heart, and with all thy soul, and with all thy mind. And thou shalt love thy public as thyself . . . All human relationships have in them something monstrous and cruel. But the relationship of the artist to the public is amongst the most monstrous."' And after a while he continues:

'But do not imagine . . . that I have no compassion on the public, or am not aware of my guilt towards them . . . I have had to read the book of Job, to get strength to bear my responsibility at all.'

'Do you see yourself in the place of Job, Charlie?' asked Æneas.

'No,' said Charlie solemnly and proudly, 'in the place of the Lord.'

'I have behaved to my reader,' he went on slowly, 'as the Lord behaved to Job.'[1]

In his essay, 'Religion, Poetry and the "Dilemma" of the Modern Writer', David Daiches points out that the central problem raised by the book of Job is that of theodicy, of the justice of the ways of God to men, and that this has long been a central theme in literature. 'The answer,' says Daiches, 'is generally given in terms of attitude rather than of logic. Job's problem disappears in a note of wonder—wonder at the grandeur and immensity of creation.'[2] This is the course adopted by a writer like Milton, for example, who answers the questions posed by religion mainly in literary or aesthetic terms. Isak Dinesen also offers an answer in terms of an attitude and of an aesthetic concept, even if it is a more self-consciously elaborated and explicative aesthetic. She herself gave the reason for the frequent references to the book of Job found in her work in one sentence. Describing the Africans in *Out of Africa*, she writes that when they speak of the personality of God, they do so 'like the last chapters of the book of Job; it is the same quality, the infinite power of imagination, with which they are impressed'.[3]

[1] *Winter's Tales*, pp. 289–291.
[2] *Literary Essays*, Edinburgh, 1956, p. 207.
[3] *Out of Africa*, p. 23.

It is this quality which also impresses her, and lies at the heart of her conception of the artist's function and of the part played by the imaginative faculties.

The artist and God are akin in the power of the imagination they both possess, even if that of God is greater. God and the imagination are really synonymous terms for Isak Dinesen. When God speaks out of the whirlwind to Job, He pleads, says Charlie 'the defence of the artist and of the artist only'. In fact He simply proclaims the omnipotence of His own imagination, and does not even attempt to justify the treatment meted out to Job in any moral or logical terms. And in the same way that God, in His behaviour to Job, asserts a majesty that may not be questioned, so too is the artist vindicated in his treatment of his characters and of the reader. Art thus becomes ultimately a religion, and the artist himself is turned into a surrogate for God, omniscient and all-powerful in the world he has created by his edict. And his word is not to be gainsaid. All tribulation is finally justified by the revelation of the design, and by the quality of the artist's imagination displayed through this revelation. The parallel this suggests with her own life is obvious. Moreover, if it is the fact that she saw life as a paradigm of art which ultimately determines the aesthetic form of her tales, this also has a concomitant effect. For the truth is that Isak Dinesen believes that life can be understood—and only fully understood— by the analogy it offers with art. We are, all of us, artists, creating the story of our lives in the very process of living, and striving to grasp its full significance through our imaginative faculties.

The artist in his work is like God in creation—indeed, according to one of the aphorisms she wrote among the notes for *Albondocani*, he becomes God: 'It is blasphemous to introduce God into novels and writing (the writer *is* God).' This belief opens a further perspective. We have noted previously that she uses the omniscient author technique in such a way that the reader never forgets her presence as the story-teller; that she continually interposes the *persona* of the narrator between us and the narration of events; and that our awareness of these qualities is sharpened by her distinctive idiom. But in the light of this belief we can see that these aspects of her narrative technique are all parts of a much more comprehensive scheme of ideas. The fullness of creation witnesses to the presence and the glory of a supreme power—whether it be God or the artist. If God is the Supreme Author, the author himself is God made everywhere manifest in his creative work. Isak Dinesen's narrative technique is not one chosen only because it best suited her genius; it constitutes an indivisible part of what she has to say. It is, in reality, a means of expressing her fundamental belief about the artist's supreme power, and of keeping the reader aware of this: through the form itself of the tales her creed is expressed and its validity demonstrated.

The situation of the artist tallies with that of God at further points. In 'The Cardinal's First Tale', the Lord catechises the artist-priest before his ordination:

> 'You are aware,' he said, 'that I am almighty. And you have before you the world which I have created. Now give me your opinion on it. Do you take it that I have meant to create a peaceful world?' 'No, my Lord,' the candidate replied. 'Or that I have,' the Lord asked, 'meant to create a pretty and neat world?' 'No, indeed,' answered the youth. 'Or a world easy to live in?' asked the Lord. 'O, good Lord, no!' said the candidate. 'Or do you,' the Lord asked for the last time, 'hold and believe that I have resolved to create a sublime world, with all things necessary to the purpose in it, and none left out?' 'I do,' said the young man. 'Then,' said the Master, 'then, My servant and mouthpiece, take the oath!'[1]

In the same way Isak Dinesen does not create a neat and pretty world, not a peaceful one, nor one easy to live in. And this needs stressing, since, although the world of her fiction does offer a release from actuality, it is neither an escape into an idealised state of existence nor a flight into an easier sphere of life. Nevertheless, she does in a very definite sense create a sublime world of the imagination, remote from ordinary life, with all things necessary for understanding it, and with nothing left out.

As God fashioned man to work out the divine purpose, so too the artist fashions his characters to work out a story. In order to

[1] *Last Tales*, pp. 21–22.

do this God has need of man ('it is even doubtful,' says Charlie Despard, 'whether the Lord is not more dependent upon Job than Job upon the Lord'); in the same way the artist has need of his characters. And just as God moves in a mysterious way his wonders to perform, so also does the artist—indeed to create a sense of mystery is one of his major functions.

The final analogy with God is the most far-reaching of all, and it is one which shows that in this aspect Isak Dinesen's work must be seen as contributing its part to what is possibly one of the chief endeavours of art in our time—the attempt to find an aesthetic equivalent for a Christian tradition regarded as moribund. At the beginning of 'The Young Man with the Carnation' Charlie Despard's situation in life is like that of Job's. 'The love of God and the certainty that in return God loved him beyond other human beings, had upheld him in times of poverty and adversity . . . But now he felt that God had turned away from him. . . . He had become estranged from God, and how was he now to live?'[1] At the end, God speaks to him in the same terms as he spoke to Job and reveals the fullest extent of his imaginative design; Charlie is reconciled to his lot and understands God's purpose—but only because his own imagination has been re-awakened. Similarly, Isak Dinesen believes that the questioning of God's purpose by Job is caused by a lack of understanding resulting from a failure of the imagination to comprehend God's ways with mankind. When God at last reveals the whole scope of his plan of creation, Job can then say with humility: 'Who is he that hideth counsel without knowledge? therefore have I uttered that I understood not; things too wonderful for me, which I knew not.'

It is the same answer we are made to give; we become as Job. For Isak Dinesen, only by the exercise of the imagination, in life, as well as in art, can we comprehend the design, understand the purpose of our existence—and be reconciled to our lot. This is the full extent of the function and the importance of imagination for her.

[1] *Winter's Tales*, pp. 5–6.

5

Art and Dream

All her life Isak Dinesen was, in Keats' phrase from 'The Fall of
Hyperion', one of 'the dreamer tribe'. 'I have the great good luck
in life,' she wrote in *Shadows on the Grass*, 'that when I sleep I
dream, and my dreams are always beautiful.'[1] At one period
alone these dreams touched on reality: 'Only during one time of
my life, and only in connection with one kind of place and
people, have phenomena of an outer world found their way into
my dreams.' Apart, however, from this single exception (and
it is not difficult to guess what period she is referring to), the
world she experienced in her dream was one utterly divorced
from that of reality: 'I move in a world deeply and sweetly
familiar to me, a world which belongs to me and to which I
myself belong more intensely than is ever the case in my waking
existence.'[2] From these scattered comments it is clear that art
and dream are really analogous states for Isak Dinesen, and
indeed she has said as much in another of her allusions to the
Book of Job:

> . . . we have in the dream forsaken our allegiance to the organising,
> controlling and rectifying forces of the world, the Universal Con-
> science. We have sworn fealty to the wild, incalculable, creative
> forces, the Imagination of the Universe. To the Conscience of the
> world we may address ourselves in prayer, it will faithfully reward
> its faithful servants . . . To the imagination of the world we do not
> pray. We call to mind how, when last we did so, we were asked
> back, quick as lightning, where we had been when the morning
> stars sang together, or whether we could bind the sweet influences

[1] op. cit., p. 107.
[2] ibid., p. 108–109.

of Pleiades. Without us having asked them for freedom these free forces have set us free as mountain winds, have liberated us from initiative and determination as from responsibility.[1]

For her, art and dreams possess a truth of their own, offer a freedom from moral imperatives and a release from actuality by creating a realm in which the truth of the imagination becomes the supreme reality. These basic assumptions underlie all Isak Dinesen's work, but 'The Dreaming Child' is one of the two stories directly concerned with showing the nature of the world which the artist-dreamer creates.

The boy, Jens—the dreaming child of the title—is brought up in a slum in Copenhagen by his foster-mother; lonely and un-cared for in these surroundings, he takes refuge in a dream-world where he imagines his real home to be in one of the great houses in the wealthy part of the town. Eventually he is adopted by a young childless couple living there, Jakob and Emilie Vandamm. Emilie, the daughter of a Copenhagen bourgeois family, had once been in love with a young naval officer, Charlie Dreyer, who had begged to be allowed to stay the night with her on the eve of his departure for a voyage to the Far East. Out-raged, she refused, soon after had married Jakob, and Charlie Dreyer had died of fever in the West Indies.

The main characteristic she is given in the story is a high moral rectitude coupled with a scrupulous regard for the truth. In this respect she is different from her easy-going husband, who is so credulous that he is taken in by any hard-luck story. As a result, he decides to adopt Jens after he has come across him in the slums and taken pity upon him. Despite her initial resistance to the idea, Emilie eventually agrees:

> 'What an absurd person you are, Jakob,' she said, 'you will believe everything that these people tell you—not because you cannot help it, but because you do really wish to believe them.'
> 'Do you not wish to believe them?' he asked her.
> 'I cannot see,' she replied, 'how one can well wish to believe or not to believe. I wish to find out the truth. Once a thing is not true,' she added, 'it matters little to me whatever else it may be.'[2]

[1] *Shadows on the Grass*, pp. 110–111.
[2] *Winter's Tales*, pp. 163–164.

One of the main themes of the tale is to show the change in Emilie's attitude to the truth under the influence of the dreamer, and to show how she is compelled to admit the existence of a form of truth higher than strict literal accuracy.

When Jens comes to their house, not only has his dream-world become real, but his powers of fantasy are so strong that he is able for a time to transform reality itself so that it takes on the semblance of his dream. 'Jens took possession of the mansion in Bredgade, and brought it to submission, neither by might nor by power, but in the quality of that fascinating and irresistible personage, perhaps the most fascinating and irresistible in the whole world: the dreamer whose dreams come true.'[1] The only person who remains impervious to Jens's spell is Emilie—conscious of the falsity of the situation since she is not his true mother. At first Jens is perfectly happy; eventually, however, he falls ill, grows gradually worse, and finally dies. After his death, Emilie is changed, she confesses to her husband that she had had a love-affair with Charlie Dreyer, and maintains that she had not sent him away that night, and that Jens had really been their child. The story finishes thus: '"Only in one thing," she said slowly, "am I wiser than you. I know that it would be better, much better, and easier for both you and me, if you would believe me." Jakob was accustomed to take a quick summary of a situation, and to make his dispositions accordingly. . . . "Yes, my dear," he said, "that is true".'

Various interpretations have been placed on this ending, and one of them in particular is significant. Aage Henriksen believed that the true interpretation was that Jens really was Charlie Dreyer's son by another woman, a prostitute, to whom he had gone immediately after leaving Emilie. In a sense therefore Jens is also Emilie's son, vicariously.[2] After his essay was first published, Isak Dinesen wrote to him, and in the letter (included

---

[1] *Winter's Tales*, p. 171. In an essay on Isak Dinesen's work by Johannes Rosendahl, a Danish critic, he quotes her as saying that the inspiration for this story came from Kipling's poem, 'The Fairies' Siege' (*Karen Blixen*, Copenhagen, 1957, p. 26). The phrase, 'The Dreamer whose dreams come true', is used as a refrain in that poem.

[2] In the essay *Karen Blixen og Marionetterne*. The essay is included in *Det guddommelige Barn*, pp. 9–32.

by Aage Henriksen as a footnote to a later edition of the essay) she remarked, 'I have not thought of the child, Jens . . . as being Charlie Dreyer's son,'[1] and added, for good measure, that she would have been interested to hear his reasons for this interpretation. This seems conclusive enough, particularly when one notes a broad hint early in the story that, except for providing some money for Jens's support, 'the father of the child . . . is otherwise unknown to this tale.' On the other hand, Johannes Rosendahl quotes Isak Dinesen as saying:

> The problem of this story is the very old one: 'What is truth?' Was not Charlie's child the only one Emilie could have—or which she did have? . . . The dreaming child is the main character because he is really the one who gives the code-word to his surroundings, the key to reality—as the dreamer always does, in fact. In this higher reality Jens really *was* the child of Emilie and Charlie, and in this fact, Emilie finds harmony in her life.[2]

These remarks are particularly interesting for the discrepancy they show when compared with the comment made to Aage Henriksen. Jens was not really Charlie Dreyer's son, but in a higher reality he *was*. If the problem of the story is 'what is truth', this only serves to show how many different sides truth has for Isak Dinesen: the facts say one thing, but the author decrees another, true only in a higher reality. It is not only the dreamer, Jens, who can alter reality and change its nature, so too can the artist in his work. Truth resides in our dreams, in our imagination, and in that of the artist's, and imaginative truth', is greater and more charged with meaning than factual everyday reality.

'Jens is the main character,' Isak Dinesen said, 'who gives the key to reality.' Just as Emilie has one predominant characteristic in the story, so also has Jens: 'The essence of his nature was longing,' and he can live only in the sphere of the imagination. His life in his new home and the reality which his former dreams have now assumed 'were all of the greatest moment because they went to prove the veracity of his visions, they were

[1] *Det guddommelige Barn*, pp. 21–22.
[2] *Karen Blixen*, pp. 25–26.

infinitely valuable as embodiments of his dreams. But within themselves they hardly meant anything to him, and they had no power to hold him. He was neither a worldling nor a struggler. He was a poet.'[1] The poet and the visionary dreamer are of the same tribe. Unlike Keats, for whom they become 'sheer antipodes', Isak Dinesen accepts this identification and makes no distinction between the creative artist, on the one hand, who in 'The Fall of Hyperion' is said 'to pour out a balm upon the world,' and the mere dreamer, on the other, who only 'vexes' it with useless visions.[2] 'What benefit canst thou or all thy tribe Do to the great world?'—the question posed by Moneta evokes a very different response from Isak Dinesen: 'I belong to an ancient, idle, wild and useless tribe.' Nor is she alone in this belief. 'All art is quite useless', Oscar Wilde asserted in the preface to *The Picture of Dorian Gray*, with his usual fondness for a startling and provocative paradox, 'no artist desires to prove anything. Even things that are true can be proved.' Isak Dinesen would go most of the way with him; for her, art (like dreams) has no pragmatic value, its justification must be sought in the fact that it creates another and more exalted mode of reality.

Because Jens lives entirely in his imagination, he has no roots in real life, and when his dreams have been completely fulfilled, he dies:

There are some young trees which, when they are planted have the root twisted, and will never take hold in the soil. They may shoot out a profusion of leaves and flowers, but they must soon die. Such was the way with Jens. He had sent out his small branches upwards and to the sides, had fared excellently of the chameleon's dish and eaten air, promise-crammed, and the while he had forgotten to put

[1] *Winter's Tales*, p. 176.
[2] In *Keats*, New York, 1955, pp. 238 ff. Middleton Murry argues cogently that Keats really meant to cancel these lines, 187–210, since they 'are irrelevant to his new condition'. 'He did not admit that he was a mere dreamer... Had he not utterly rejected dreams? Did he not know that he was a true poet? . . . The first great reason why Keats cancelled the lines and why they must remain cancelled is that they were not true of himself.' They may, however, be true in general, and be true of Keats himself prior to the second *Hyperion*, or even up to the point in that poem where he learns from Moneta to reject dreams.

out roots . . . It is possible, had his imagination been turned on to fresh pastures, that he might for a while have drawn nourishment through it, and have delayed his exit.[1]

The same image is also used in 'The Dreamers', the other story having a similar subject:

'You know, Tembu,' said Mira suddenly, after a pause, 'that if, in planting a coffee tree, you bend the taproot, that tree will start, after a little time, to put out a multitude of small delicate roots near the surface. That tree will never thrive, nor bear fruit, but it will flower more richly than the others.

'Those fine roots are the dreams of the tree. As it puts them out, it need no longer think of its bent taproot. It keeps alive by them— a little, not very long. Or you can say that it dies by them, if you like. For really, dreaming is the well-mannered people's way of committing suicide.'[2]

If Isak Dinesen was a dreamer by nature, and if dreams were the source of one of her greatest joys, she was nevertheless aware of a tantalising paradox. The poet-dreamer is set apart from ordinary life; he can indeed transform reality by animating it with his imagination, but any attempt to bring art or dream closer to actuality is doomed to failure, leaving a cold inanimate world with nothing in it to sustain the imagination. The artist-dreamer cannot bear too much reality: he is condemned to live in a state of tantalised longing for his dreams to be fulfilled—a fulfilment which he is ever denied. Again the difference this suggests from Keats is apparent. In 'The Fall of Hyperion' Keats tries to move his art away from profitless dreams and closer to human life and human reality by seeking for a way to accommodate 'the miseries of the world' within it; Isak Dinesen, on the other hand, pursues a course diametrically opposed. She endeavours to secure her art against any stained contagion from the world, and to preserve the artist-dreamer in a pure and unsullied state. What is life for Keats constitutes only death of the imaginative spirit for her.

One final point remains. 'The Dreaming Child' turns upon

[1] *Winter's Tales*, p. 177.
[2] *Seven Gothic Tales*, p. 277.

the poles of truth, and the story pivots around the difference between the everyday world and the dream. But the difference remains throughout merely an abstract statement and does not become a concrete demonstration within the terms of the story: there is really little or no attempt to give Jens's vision a clearer definition. We are told, for example, that one effect of the spell, which Jens, as a dreamer, cast over his new home, was that 'people were made to see themselves with the eyes of the dreamer, and were impelled to live up to an ideal, and that for this their higher existence, they became dependent upon him.'[1] But this is not really so. They neither wholly see themselves in this way, nor indeed are they seen from this viewpoint by the reader: we see them through a narrator's eyes as characters in a story, not as figures in a dreamer's vision. Moreover, the change Jens causes in Emilie occurs quite suddenly after his death, and his whole dream during his life has had little impact either upon her or upon the reader. We have to accept its invincible power as an unsubstantiated fact decreed by the author.

The contrast all this offers with 'The Dreamers' is a striking one: the same themes are treated there, but with a skill and artistry which gives a density of texture and an imaginative complexity to the story, that bear further witness to the drastic schematisation of 'The Dreaming Child'. The opening and closing scenes take place on board a dhow off the east coast of Africa; these two brief scenes frame the whole inset narrative, told by one of the main characters, Lincoln Forsner, to Mira Jama, who is sailing with him. His story concerns Pellegrina Leoni, the greatest opera-singer of her day, who had dedicated her entire life to the service of her art. She had two great passions; one was her love for her audience, the other was 'her passion for the great soprano, Pellegrina Leoni. . . . She worked in the service of Pellegrina Leoni like a slave under the whip.'[2] In a fire that broke out one evening in the theatre she was injured so seriously that she would never be able to sing again. The tap-root of her existence having been broken, she decides,

[1] *Winter's Tales*, p. 172.
[2] *Seven Gothic Tales*, pp. 332–333.

after she has recovered from her injuries, that it must be given out that she has died, and asks Marcus Cocoza, her patron and friend, to arrange this. 'Pellegrina is dead,' she said . . . 'You must now help me to tell the world of her death . . . Nobody, nobody must ever be Pellegrina again. To have her once more upon the stage of life, of this hard world, and to have such awful things happen to her as do happen to people on earth—no, that must not be thought of.'[1]

One notices here a peculiarity in her mode of speaking: Pellegrina refers to herself in the third person, giving the effect that she is talking about a different person. And this is really the case. The disaster has given her an added awareness of the identity she had previously had as the opera-singer Pellegrina Leoni at the same time as it has cruelly and irrevocably deprived her of this identity. Armed with this new self-knowledge, she decides what her next step should be:

> 'I will not be one person again, Marcus, I will always be many persons from now. Never again will I have my heart and my whole life bound up with one woman, to suffer so much.' . . . 'And you, Marcus,' . . . 'now I shall give you this good advice. Be many people. . . . You have worried too much about Marcus Cocoza, so that you have been really his slave and his prisoner . . . You must, from now, be more than one, many people, as many as you can think of. I feel, Marcus,—I am sure—that all people in the world ought to be, each of them, more than one.'[2]

The similarity this offers with Isak Dinesen herself does not need stressing—except that her own situation and Pellegrina's are reversed. Whereas Pellegrina ceases to be an artist, and moves into life, having lost her voice, Isak Dinesen, by moving into the sphere of art, and becoming a writer, found hers. From now on Pellegrina assumes a series of masks as a means of defence; in all her protean identities she is only very little concerned, regardless of what happens. She has, in fact, become detached from 'the stage of life, of this hard world' in the same

[1] *Seven Gothic Tales*, p. 344.
[2] ibid., p. 345.

way that an actor is detached from the role he is playing.[1] But there is one great compensation: under these conditions her imagination has been liberated, and she is free to play whatever role she chooses by assuming any identity which appeals to her fancy. Moreover, these masks need only be dependent upon the quality of the imagination with which she is able to envisage them.

Her effect as a singer is described by Marcus thus: 'I understood the meaning of heaven and earth, of the stars, life and death, and eternity.'[2] Lincoln Forsner knew her as the woman, Olalla, with whom, in Rome, he fell passionately in love. Suddenly, with no warning at all, she left him, but he tells Mira Jama that he realises that 'to this woman I owe it that I have ever understood . . . the meaning of such words as tears, heart, longing, stars, which you poets make use of.'[3] Nor is this feeling of exaltation confined solely to Lincoln; she has a similar effect on all the other men who knew her, each of them, under a different alias. She exercises, in fact, the same effect in life, through the different identities she assumes, as she did when she was an artist. In her role as Olalla she rouses Lincoln's imagination so that he is taught to dream, and the dream is the story he tells Mira Jama.

His story about Pellegrina is told twenty years after it had all happened. In reading it we are kept continually aware of this retrospective view, since 'The Dreamers' not only starts and finishes on the dhow, but Lincoln also frequently breaks off his own tale to refer to Mira Jama and to bring the reader back to the present time of the narrator. Thus the move back into the past, when he again picks up the thread of his narrative, is accentuated. The way in which the story continually weaves back and forth between past and present plays an essential part since, in contrast to Isak Dinesen's usual technique, we see

[1] One is again reminded of Yeats using the mask as a defence against a hostile world. As Richard Ellmann says, wearing a mask, 'we are only slightly involved . . . This theory seems to assume that we can be detached from experience like actors from a play.' (*Yeats: The Man and the Masks*, p. 176.)
[2] *Seven Gothic Tales*, p. 331.
[3] ibid., pp. 282–283.

these events (and are continually reminded of this fact) through the eyes of a main character—one who has become a dreamer *before* the story starts. This both colours Lincoln's story and is meant to colour our response to it. 'The Dreamers', in other words, demands an energy of response from the reader that really does vitalise his imagination. The tale is not intended to be a representation of reality, nor even to give the slightest illusion of being so; on the contrary, it shows how Lincoln, the dreamer, envisions reality, and only that. In 'The Dreaming Child' Jens's vision and dream remains simply a postulate; here it is Lincoln's dream itself which, by a simple but effective change in the narrative technique, affords both the substance of the story and demonstrates the imaginative powers of the dreamer. And this is achieved partly by the fact that Lincoln Forsner's personality is refined down to one single trait, and partly by the form of the tale—for Lincoln's story is actually endowed with all the characteristics of a dream.

It is this that explains, for example, the full significance of Lincoln's thoughts after hearing the story of his friend, Pilot, about Madame Lola, another of Pellegrina's identities: 'This tale of my friend's,' he thinks, 'is too much like a dream of my own.'[1] Madame Lola had been the leader of a group of revolutionaries in Lucerne; Pilot had become involved with them, fought during an uprising on the barricades by Madame Lola's side, and had been struck down in the hand-to-hand fighting. She had nursed him back to health, and kept him in hiding, since he was, so she had said, wanted by the authorities for having killed someone during the revolt. Then, with the help of Marcus Cocoza, she had smuggled him out of the town, and he had never seen her since. Now he is searching for her and, in a hotel high up in the Swiss Alps, meets Lincoln on the same quest. But if Lincoln feels that Pilot's story is unreal and like a dream he himself has had, it is also very apparent to the reader that Pilot himself has been made to imagine much in the whole episode. He has overheard himself described as a *golem* by Marcus. 'Then I did not know what I found out later, that the

---

[1] *Seven Gothic Tales*, p. 303.

word *golem*, in the Jewish language, means a big figure of clay, into which life is magically blown, most frequently for the accomplishment of some crime which the magician dares not undertake himself.'[1]

In a hotel, while Pilot, Lincoln and another character, a Swedish Baron, sit talking of the woman they are all in search of, quite suddenly and with no warning, Marcus Cocoza appears. 'Whatever magic I had encountered was encircling them as well as me,' Lincoln thinks, on observing that the other two had also recognised him, 'or else they were themselves creatures of my imagination.'[2] Using the dream-form as her method of narrating 'The Dreamers', Isak Dinesen thus makes the form its main point. This can be seen most clearly when the Baron is interrupted by Pilot in his tale of the woman he knew in the guise of Rosalba (the Baron's story, again in the way of dreams, is never rounded off, but simply merges into another episode). Lincoln thinks:

I am dreaming. By now I am quite sure that I am dreaming. This hotel, Pilot, and the Swedish Baron are all parts of a dream. Good God, what a nightmare! I have at last lost my reason for good and all, and the next thing that will happen will be that Olalla will walk in through that door, swiftly, as she always comes in dreams. With that thought I kept my eyes on the door. From time to time while we have been talking, new guests had come in from the outside . . . Now a lady and her maid came in, and passed us quickly and quietly.[3]

This reappearance of Pellegrina on the scene is quite unmotivated: such a thing could only happen in dreams, Lincoln thinks—and then it does. Lincoln himself is a dreamer wrapt in an imaginary world of his own devising. The episode shows how diametrically opposed to reality Lincoln's story is, and the very distance from reality, preserved throughout, becomes a way of measuring the whole tale's achievement.

A remoteness from reality has, however, at least one major

[1] *Seven Gothic Tales*, p. 302.
[2] ibid., p. 303.
[3] ibid., pp. 312–313.

disadvantage. In the kind of posthumous existence which Pellegrina creates for herself after her accident, she is able to assume other identities—but only for a time. She asks Marcus to act as a kind of *deus ex machina* so that, if anyone should ever guess her secret and suspect that she really is Pellegrina, he can help her get away in time before the truth finally comes out. He has done this on several previous occasions, but, in the end, even he is powerless to prevent this from happening. Pellegrina flees from Lincoln and the other two men, up into the mountain passes, but they catch up with her and demand to know who she really is. She tries to elude them again, but in the attempt, is fatally injured in a fall down the cliff-side. Her flight of fancy has been brought down to earth, and in the end it is reality that triumphs.

The implication of this is personified in Mira Jama: he is both a listener—and a warning. Formerly he had been a storyteller, but is so no longer. The reasons he gives Lincoln for the failure of his creative imagination have a direct bearing on Isak Dinesen's whole concept of the dream and the state of imagination it represents: 'When you know what things are really like, you can make no poems about them . . . I have become too familiar with life.'[1] The men who pursue Pellegrina to her death also want to know what things are really like and to discover the truth; Jens became too familiar with life and died. The remoteness of dreams and the distance of realm of the imagination from ordinary life are the prime conditions for their survival—as it is for the artist as well.

We have already noted the significance of the Book of Job for Isak Dinesen in revealing the infinite power of the imagination. But there is also another book that has the same appeal. When the Africans talk of the personality of God, she says that they sound not only like the last chapters of Job, 'they speak like the Arabian Nights'.[2] There are several allusions to this book in her tales, and her intricate technique as a storyteller (amply demonstrated by 'The Dreamers') has sometimes been compared to Scheherazade's. But it is also possible to see an even more

[1] *Seven Gothic Tales*, p. 274.
[2] *Out of Africa*, p. 23.

fundamental similarity. Scheherazade used her imagination to hold the world and everyday life at bay; Isak Dinesen does the same, by setting her stories in the past, by investing them with a high degree of fantasy—or by investing them with all the semblance of dreams.

6

The Revenge of Truth

The play entitled *Sandhedens Hævn*[1] was written in Danish
when Isak Dinesen was a girl, performed by the young Dinesen
family at Rungstedlund, and published many years later, in
1926, in *Tilskueren*. It occurs both directly and indirectly in her
tales: a passage from it is quoted almost verbatim, for example,
in 'The Roads round Pisa',[2] where it offers a key to that story,
and it is directly alluded to in another.[3] In 1960 it was repub-
lished in Denmark as a small volume; during the last ten years
it has been performed at various theatres in Scandinavia and it
has also been shown on Danish, German and Italian television.
No English version exists of the play, although Miss Svendsen
wrote to me that 'a few months before her death Isak Dinesen
had begun a translation because one of her agents was eager to
have an English version available. But it was very difficult for
her to go back to such an early work, she felt somehow that it
was not good enough to translate, and the effort came to an end
after a few pages.' Even though this judgement may very well be
true, *The Revenge of Truth* is still of considerable interest. It is
subtitled 'a marionette comedy', and critics who have written at
any length about Isak Dinesen have stressed the prominence of
the marionette theme in her work as a whole. Aage Henriksen is
probably the one who has pursued this in most detail in two
essays published in 1952,[4] which trace a similarity between this

[1] See Appendix for an English translation.
[2] *Seven Gothic Tales*, pp. 199–200.
[3] 'When they were children the young De Conincks had lived under a
special superstition, which they had from a marionette comedy. It came to
this: that the lies you tell are likely to become truth.' ('The Supper at
Elsinore', *Seven Gothic Tales*, p. 257.)
[4] *Karen Blixen og Marionetterne*.

concept in her work and that found in Heinrich von Kleist's dialogue about puppets, '*Über das Marionettentheater*', written around the beginning of the nineteenth century. In this the narrator has been surprised several times to see a well-known dancer, obviously fascinated, watching puppets performing in an open-air marionette theatre. Asked the reason for his fascination, the dancer replies that puppets have one enormous advantage over human performers—they have no soul or consciousness. As a result they enjoy the blessing of automatism and unconsciousness, respond completely to the demands of the puppet-master, and have no possibility whatsoever of playing any role independently of him. Consequently, they deliver, quite literally, their role and destiny safely into his hands. The idea implicit in both Kleist and Isak Dinesen, according to Aage Henriksen, is that each person has a particular destiny to fulfil, but that man, in contrast to the puppet, is endowed with self-consciousness, and is therefore able to thwart this destiny. What is pure blessing for the marionette becomes a very mixed one for man, since he occupies the isthmus of a middle state between the puppet with no consciousness at all, on the one hand, and God, representing consciousness infinite, on the other. Consequently man has the doubtful, even dangerous privilege of being able to live according to his own will and ideas, rather than simply carrying out God's purpose like the puppet obeying the puppet-master.[1]

Robert Langbaum also assigns a central place to the marionette theme in Isak Dinesen's work; writing about *The Revenge of Truth*, he says that 'although she was never again to use marionettes, the marionette comedy helps us to understand some of her most characteristic qualities—the deliberate emphasis on artifice and the imposition on painful material of a comic awareness, the awareness that someone is pulling the

[1] Although further consideration of this is not strictly relevant here, it should perhaps be pointed out that this interpretation does not exhaust the significance of Kleist's essay. Wellek, for example, sees it as a defence of unconscious creation, of a basic irrationalism in art. (René Wellek: *A History of Modern Criticism*, Vol. II, New Haven, 1955, pp. 290–291). This aspect is obviously very far removed from Isak Dinesen. Kleist's essay can, of course, also be read as an analysis of the psychology of the theatre and of acting.

strings, as an answer to the story's problems.'[1] Eric Johannesson, however, goes furthest of all in his interpretation of its significance: 'To Dinesen,' he remarks, *tout court*, 'life is a marionette comedy.'[2] With such unanimity on the importance of this theme, it is worth examining it in some detail in *The Revenge of Truth*.

The play takes place at an inn in Holland where Abraham, the innkeeper, makes a living by murdering the guests and stealing their belongings with the help of his accomplice Mopsus, the potman. He plans to do the same with Jan Bravida, the hero, who stays overnight at the inn, but instead it is Abraham who is outwitted, and Jan Bravida escapes with Abraham's daughter, Sabine, with whom he has fallen in love. They are helped to outwit him by the fact that a witch casts a spell over everybody in the inn through which all lies told during the night are turned into the truth—truth, in fact, takes its revenge.

There are certain aspects of this play—apart from the quite fantastic nature of the plot—which immediately set a very individual stamp upon it. In one scene, for example, instead of Jan Bravida making a reply to something Mopsus has said, the following stage direction is given: 'His reply is thought to mar the scene so it is omitted.'[3] In the same scene Mopsus tries to step out of his role as a character by claiming that he is really the author of the play in which they are all acting, and that everything in it has been a great success except for his own characterisation. Therefore he is going to discard the rest of the play and improvise the action in order to bring out the main facets of his own personality. Noting that there are only seven scenes left (there are really only six), he declares: 'I'm going to sacrifice the whole plot in order to make my own character clear in those seven scenes.' And, at the end of the play, when the villain, Abraham, has lost all his ill-gotten gains, he leaves, saying, 'why should I waste more words on this audience, which doesn't understand me, and on this comedy, where everything has

---

[1] *The Gayety of Vision*, pp. 48–49.
[2] *The World of Isak Dinesen*, Seattle, 1961, p. 89.
[3] Scene II.

turned out badly for me, even though it could just as easily have turned out well. In fact everything would have been more original like that.'[1] These remarks all constitute an essential feature of the play. What this consists of is shown in the following short scene:

> *Mopsus :* You here, what are you doing here, shouldn't you be doing the washing-up?
> *Fortunio :* I'm waiting for you, we have to act in a scene together.
> *Mopsus :* Which scene is that?
> *Fortunio :* The one in which I tell you that Abraham has asked me to dig a grave in the field under the pear-tree in blossom. I ask you to help me, and we talk about life after death. It's necessary for the harmony of the plot.
> *Mopsus :* Yes, that's right, I remember that scene. It's a terribly boring one, let's skip it.[2]

The impression this gives is that the characters are really working from a scenario rather than from a completed script, and that they are thus improvising their dialogue instead of reciting the lines from a finished work. *Tonight We Improvise*, the title of Pirandello's play, could just as well have replaced 'A Marionette Comedy' as the subtitle of this one. In fact, what *The Revenge of Truth* really calls to mind is a work in the *commedia dell' arte* tradition, and there are grounds for considering it as stemming, however indirectly, from this tradition, and not for seeing it as being purely and simply a puppet-play. Several points confirm this.

When a performance of this play takes place in 'The Roads round Pisa', it is one in which the parts are acted by puppets; nevertheless, as we have noted, it was first written to be performed by live actors. Moreover, the fact that Isak Dinesen was familiar with the *commedia dell' arte* tradition in general is clear from the various references in her work to its stock persons. In 'Carnival', the characters are dressed as these figures, and in

---

[1] Scene 15.
[2] Scene 8. This scene does not appear in the extant early drafts of the play —an indication that the general tendency illustrated here was one that Isak Dinesen developed and elaborated in later versions.

another unpublished story, 'Anna', an old ballet-master, M. Dombasle, goes to the town of Bergamo because he has been told that it was here that the figure of Arlecchino had originated: 'A man of clay into whose nostrils God had breathed life.' Nor must one overlook the fact that a form of the *commedia dell' arte* still survives to this day in Copenhagen in the Pantomime Theatre in Tivoli; and in the same way that most English children at some time or other in their lives have seen *Babes in the Wood*, or *Cinderella*, or other pantomimes at Christmas, so, too, have most Danish children been taken to this theatre. Karen Dinesen was no exception to this.

Other similarities with the *commedia dell' arte* can be traced in *The Revenge of Truth*, although they are not as important as the element of apparent improvisation. Mopsus, the potman, for instance, has some of the characteristics of Arlecchino, the comic servant or clown in his original Italian form. (He is described as being 'the clown' in 'The Roads round Pisa'.) The action of the *commedia dell' arte*, often centering around the intrigue of two young lovers and the way they attain happiness and money by outwitting their elders with their servants' help, is also paralleled in *The Revenge of Truth* with the intrigue between Jan Bravida and Sabine; and they too eventually outwit Sabine's father and elope with his money. Finally, in remarking upon these similarities, it should be stressed that there are no reasons for making a sharp distinction between these aspects of the *commedia dell' arte* and the puppet-play elements; they are not mutually exclusive, but merge into each other within *The Revenge of Truth*. And the way they do this in the play also reflects—but to a greater extent—the connection sometimes found between the two traditions. The way in which Punch in the Punch-and-Judy puppet show ultimately derives from Pulcinella is but one example of this.

However, the general importance of the *commedia dell' arte* tradition with Isak Dinesen extends far beyond the specific parallels to it found in *The Revenge of Truth*. In fact, the *commedia dell' arte* in many ways represents an analogue of her attitude to life, which is much subtler and more complex than one which merely sees life in terms of the puppet and puppet-master. And again one can see that the writer with whom she has most affinities in this respect is W. B. Yeats. Explaining some of the more esoteric terms in his philosophy, Yeats wrote:

> When I wish for some general idea which will describe the Great Wheel as an individual life I go to the *Commedia dell' Arte* or improvised drama of Italy. The stage-manager, or *Daïmon*, offers his actor an inherited scenario, the *Body of Fate*, and a *Mask* or role as unlike as possible to his natural ego or *Will*, and leaves him to improvise through his *Creative Mind* the dialogue and details of the plot. He must discover or reveal a being which only exists with extreme effort, when his muscles are as it were all taut and all his energies active.[1]

The ideas in Isak Dinesen follow these very closely. In the *commedia dell' arte* the function of the playwright is restricted to composing the framework of the plot; the actors themselves become their own authors, improvising their action and dialogue from this scenario. Isak Dinesen likewise believes that every person has the possibility of improvising the details of his individual life, of playing his part, and thus of fulfilling his destiny within the general framework provided by God. The actor in the *commedia dell' arte* frequently donned a mask both to signify he was playing a role and to indicate its nature; this is also what a person can do in life—whether the mask is called 'Isak Dinesen' or some other name. As the actor on the stage in the *commedia dell' arte* had a role assigned to him, so has each person in life, and the way the role of a Pellegrina or of an Isak Dinesen is carried out, if acted splendidly enough, rises supremely over all questions of factual truth or sincerity. Her attitude is really the same as that expressed in Santayana's outburst in *Soliloquies in England*, and it is one which takes us to the heart of Isak Dinesen's most tenaciously held beliefs:

> What . . . could be more splendidly sincere than the impulse to play in real life, to rise on the rising wave of every feeling and let it burst, if it will, into the foam of exaggeration? Life is not a means, the mind is not a slave nor a photograph: it has a right to enact a pose, to assume a *panache*, and to create what prodigious allegories

[1] *A Vision*, New York, 1961, pp. 83–84.

it will for the mere sport and glory of it. . . . To embroider upon experience is not to bear false witness against one's neighbour, but to bear true witness to oneself.[1]

Man *does* have a choice; he can either choose to play the role which has been sketched out for him, whole-heartedly, with style, *panache* and imagination, or he can refuse to do so, in which case he is not an actor, but becomes merely a spectator. This possibility of choice, far from being a doubtful privilege as with Kleist, is really, for Isak Dinesen, man's crowning one. In one of her most eloquent passages she gave expression to these ideas, and to her awareness of the potentialities inherent in the choice with which man is faced:

> Pride is faith in the idea that God had, when he made us. A proud man is conscious of the idea, and aspires to realize it. He does not strive towards a happiness, or comfort, which may be irrelevant to God's idea of him. His success is the idea of God, successfully carried through, and he is in love with his destiny. As the good citizen finds his happiness in the fulfilment of his duty to the community, so does the proud man find his happiness in the fulfilment of his fate.
>
> People who have no pride are not aware of any idea of God in the making of them, and sometimes they make you doubt that there has ever been much of an idea, or else it has been lost, and who shall find it again? They have got to accept as success what others warrant to be so, and to take their happiness, and even their own selves, at the quotation of the day. They tremble, with reason, before their fate.[2]

To become completely conscious of this idea and to aspire to realize it—these are man's primary functions; and both of them are very far removed from the unconscious state and the mechanical automatism represented by the puppet.

In 'Carnival', the character, Mimi, recalls some of the people she knew as a child:

'Do you remember those people who were old when we were children,—the nuns at the French school, and our maiden aunts,—

[1] *Soliloquies in England and Later Soliloquies*, New York, 1923, p. 138.
[2] *Out of Africa*, p. 261.

who believed in God?—They lived in God, and threw themselves upon the Lord, and rested in him, and all that. Now say that that was the thing which God disliked most of all, and that in the end he would say to them: "For the love of God,"—or whatever words he uses to that effect,—"Do think of something to do for yourselves, find some interest of your own in life. I really should not have created you if I had known that you could do nothing but fall back upon me again." '

To fulfil one's destiny by realising God's intentions does not entail a passive surrender to God's will, nor does it mean 'falling back upon him', and allowing oneself to be animated solely by the great puppet-master who, by manipulating the strings and controlling every action, makes us dance to his will. On the contrary, it demands an active co-operation with God, a co-operation like that between the scenario-writer and the *commedia dell' arte* performers, who dramatised and brought to imaginative life the roles they had been allotted.

When reading through the observations on pride in the passage from *Out of Africa*, one notices how deeply it is imbued with religious feeling. And in considering this aspect of Isak Dinesen's thought, it is equally obvious that we are again coming very close to a principle which does for her amount to a religious one. Her works are studded with references to God and to fate or destiny, and yet it is clear (even from what has been said so far about the freedom each person has to choose whether or not to play his role in life and thus fulfil his destiny) that the idea behind these concepts cannot strictly be described as a determinist one. Nor, on the other hand, can the concept of God as being 'the Arbiter of the Masquerade', to use a phrase from 'The Deluge at Norderney',[1] be described as primarily a Christian one. Nevertheless, Isak Dinesen does believe in God—but God as a metaphor rather than a fact. Her attitude is indeed very like that revealed in a remark made by the actor, Emmanuelson, in *Out of Africa*. She asked him if he believed in God, and he replied, 'perhaps you will think me a terrible sceptic. . . . But with the exception of God I believe in absolutely nothing

[1] *Seven Gothic Tales*, p. 26.

whatever.'[1] How closely this tallies with her own belief is shown in *Breve fra et Land i Krig*, (*Letters from a Country at War*) where she writes of an episode which happened to her in Nazi Germany when she was commissioned in 1940 by some Scandinavian newspapers to write a series of articles on the situation there. Someone asked her if she was really so out-of-date as to believe in the grace of God. '"I can answer," she replied, "like a friend of mine, a Swedish actor, answered me when I asked him if he believed in God"—"I am a terribly great sceptic," he said, "I believe in nothing else whatsoever".'[2]

The particular form Isak Dinesen's belief in God takes is crystallised in a remark to be found among her notes for *Albondocani*. 'Every human being,' she wrote, 'believes in God—*in a guiding principle in the universe*. It depends then on which God he believes in.'[3] God, in her tales, manifests himself in many guises; and the beliefs of the characters are equally multifarious. In 'Peter and Rosa', for example, Peter Købke believes that 'God means me to be a sailor' but he has not carried out God's meaning with his life: 'I have crossed his plans instead. I have worked against him, just because the people by me, such people as are called your neighbours, have wished me to do so.'[4] He has thus fallen into the second category in the passage on pride in *Out of Africa*, of those people who accept as success what others warrant to be so. Eventually, however, he decides to carry out God's design and thus moves into the first one. In a way, he does go to sea; he ventures, together with Rosa, on the ice covering the Sound between Denmark and Sweden. There on the ice-floes they meet their death, but Peter dies rejoicing that, nevertheless, he has succeeded in fulfilling his destiny.

In 'The Invincible Slave-Owners' the guiding principle in the lives of the two sisters consists in maintaining appearances before the world; to this apparently trivial end they devote their entire existence. They are 'the partisans of an ideal, ever in

[1] op. cit., p. 201.
[2] *Essays*, p. 147.
[3] My emphasis.
[4] *Winter's Tales*, p. 263.

flight from a blunt reality'.[1] In 'The Fish' Erik Klipping, King of Denmark in the thirteenth century, thinks that the concord and understanding between himself and the Lord would be perfect if only they were alone on the earth, with no other human beings to come between them and dim the perception of their concord. '"Oh, Lord, it is time," the King thought, "that I should turn away from them, that I should throw off everybody that stands in the way of the happiness of my soul . . . I will save my soul, I will feel it rejoice once more."'[2] He follows this principle, accepts the ring found in the fish as a sign of his destiny, and eventually, because of this ring and the love-affair it involves him in, perishes.[3]

The implications of the remark in Isak Dinesen's manuscripts also defines in clear and unmistakeable terms the basis on which much of her attitude to life rests. The 'guiding principle' is one, immanent and present throughout the universe as a leading and sustaining spirit. But this principle also creates an inescapable condition for man; it is the lot of each individual person to decide what exactly this principle consists of, and to follow it in his own life. This observation, written towards the end of Isak Dinesen's life, in turn leads us back to *The Revenge of Truth*, one of her earliest works.

The part of Amiane, the witch in *The Revenge of Truth*, was originally played by Karen Dinesen herself. (In the draft of her English version there is a stage direction, when the witch first appears, which reads: '*Amiane*, in costume and mask as like Isak Dinesen as possible.') Amiane appears at the beginning of the play and tells the innkeeper that she has come to tell him the truth. Challenged to do so, she replies: 'The truth is that we are

---

[1] *Winter's Tales*, p. 155.

[2] ibid., p. 229.

[3] This is the tale where Isak Dinesen is most hampered by writing a story in English while using a purely Danish frame of reference. An indication of this is the different title it has in Danish: '*Fra det gamle Danmark*' (From the Denmark of Old). She thus draws on a cluster of historical allusions not accessible to the English reader.

How much Isak Dinesen is restricted in this story is indicated by the note appended at the end to explain the Danish references. One other similar case occurs in her work, 'Converse at Night in Copenhagen' in *Last Tales*, where she is forced to resort to the same device.

all acting in a marionette comedy,' and when Abraham retorts that that is merely an old cliché, she continues:

> My children, what is more important than anything else in a marionette comedy is to keep the author's idea clear. I will tell you, even though it is a secret, that this is the real happiness which people seek everywhere else. To act in a marionette comedy is a true blessing, and now that at long last I have come into one, I will never go out of it again. But you, my fellow-actors, keep the author's idea clear. Aye, drive it to its utmost consequence.'

What she says here is obviously central, since it is the passage which is quoted in 'The Roads round Pisa', and it has also been used as a keystone in the conception of human beings as puppets attributed to her. However, the full significance of this speech can only be seen if it is placed in its context and coupled with another of the play's major characteristics—the quite striking inconsistencies apparent in it.

These can be noted from the very beginning in the *dramatis personae*. In this Jan Bravida is described as being a journalist as well as a *lansquenet*.[2] One learns during the course of the play that he is a columnist who writes theatre reviews, although it is never made clear how he manages to combine this with soldiering as a profession. Moreover, although the *lansquenets* were German and French mercenary foot-soldiers in the fifteenth to seventeenth century, the action of *The Revenge of Truth* takes place in the early twentieth.[3] The character of Mopsus, the potman, also has a quality of inconsistency, although of another sort. He is the landlord's henchman; he is also given the most

---

[1] Scene 2. This concept is expressed even more strongly in the English draft, viz.:
'The one important thing in a marionette comedy is to stick to the idea of the author, to keep the author's idea clear, to pursue the author's idea to its utmost consequence . . . That is what makes it truly pleasant to be a marionette! . . . But O you my fellow actors, I beseech you, do keep the idea of the author clear! Do pursue it to its utmost consequence!'

[2] This is the term Isak Dinesen used in her English draft.

[3] Again this is an inconsistency that is stressed in Isak Dinesen's English draft. There, Jan Bravida is described as being on his way from the siege of Bergen-op-Zoom, the town in Holland besieged and captured by the French in 1747 and again in 1795.

philosophical speeches in the play. In a play which opens with a reference to Henry Ford, Sabine dreams of keeping a horse and carriage, and the lovers elope from the inn on mules. And although the action takes place at an inn near Edam in Holland, Jan Bravida is still a frequent visitor to Klampenborg, the race-course just outside Copenhagen.

By themselves, these are all minor points, but they add up to a deliberate design when seen in conjunction with Amiane's speech setting out the play's guiding principle. For it *is* this, since Amiane is really playing the role of God. It is she who has created the play and, in addition, she performs the part of a *deus ex machina* who contrives the *dénouement* through her spell. 'We are all acting in a marionette comedy,' she says, 'and now that at long last I have come into one, I will never go out of it again.' She has, in other words, moved from life into art; they are all taking part in a marionette comedy on the stage—and are fully conscious of this fact. In thus addressing her 'fellow-actors' she is deliberately excluding the audience, as she has already done from the beginning: 'Even every individual member of the audience may be thought of as one of the ideas of Nature, although, considered as an audience, they aren't really, for there are limits to everything.'[1] This is something upon which the whole play rests, and is underlined by the other characters as well:

> *Jan Bravida:* I've got to review a première for tomorrow's paper. If you help me, Sabine, I'll finish it more quickly.
> *Sabine:* What kind of première is it?
> *Jan Bravida:* This one, Sabine. Look out there, and tell me who are sitting in the stalls.
> *Sabine:* Oh, Jan Bravida, don't talk like that. You know very well who are in the stalls.
> *Jan Bravida:* Yes, I know, and they all know. But what can we do about it.[2]

The presence of the audience is recognised throughout—as something alien to the whole play. The players exist only within

[1] Scene 2.
[2] Scene 9.

the charmed circle drawn by Amiane's arts, and within this the audience has no place. The characters have carried out the conditions imposed upon them, they have performed their parts as well as they were able, kept the author's idea clear and, by the end, they have also succeeded in discovering their identity, by becoming fully conscious of the design the author intended to draw through the roles she assigned them. The persons in a work of art are not like the audience and life, and are not meant to be, but life can become like them, and should even try to do so, by revealing through art 'a being', in Yeats's words, 'which exists only with extreme effort'. Sabine winds up the performance by saying:

> We have done our best, and we don't ask to do more than that. When we first began, no one knew what his role was like, indeed, we ourselves didn't know, for who can tell what a character will look like on the stage? But now we have said those lines we had in us, we haven't kept a single one back, and when the curtain falls, no one can have any doubt what we really were. Oh I hope that sometime each member of the audience will be able to say the same thing!

Despite the fact that the play was not published until 1926, the place of *The Revenge of Truth* is definitely among Isak Dinesen's juvenilia. Thomas Dinesen still has a very clear recollection of the performances in which he took part as a boy; even after the lapse of so many years, he could recite whole passages by heart. He thought that the published version did not differ greatly from the original, and extant manuscripts confirm this. One of them is probably written out by Isak Dinesen's sister, Ellen, and thus suggests that it dates back to the early period of family life at Rungstedlund when she also took part in the performances. This, of course, does not preclude certain changes and revisions having been made according to Isak Dinesen's usual custom, but these, as we have noted, were chiefly directed to clarifying the main themes already there from the beginning. This very early play then, first written when she was about seventeen, is rooted in the same concepts that govern all the work of her maturity. It thus provides further evidence that the later phase of her life, when she became a full-time writer, instead of bringing with it fresh ideas, found her already securely ensconced within a framework of beliefs which derives from her earlier years. If 'Isak Dinesen' marked a new start in her life, it did not really initiate anything correspondingly novel in her art. It is really strange and surely very seldom that a person who had led such an immensely full, varied and active life as Karen Blixen did, a person who laid aside writing for a period of many years, during which she was preoccupied with something utterly different, could still, when she returned to writing, preserve such an unbroken continuity of beliefs. Instead of her experience in maturity modifying the attitude to life and art of her youth shown in *The Revenge of Truth*, it serves to steel it even more.

All the elements that make up *The Revenge of Truth*—the magic spell itself which calls the play into existence, the inconsistencies, the characters' consciousness of their own roles, and their awareness of the audience, are meant to eradicate any semblance of verisimilitude and to dispel the illusion of life normally given by a play. It never demands for one moment from us that willing suspension of disbelief that for Coleridge constituted poetic faith; instead *The Revenge of Truth* firmly marks out the gulf separating art from life. Art thereby reminds us that it is art—as it always does with Isak Dinesen.

7
Art and Life

Amiane's exhortation in *The Revenge of Truth* to follow a guiding principle establishes the main theme of 'The Roads round Pisa', where the speech is quoted during a performance of the marionette comedy watched by some of the characters in the story. They have not done this, and consequently, like marionettes who have succeeded only in getting the strings entangled, they are forced into another pattern of events, which unravels these strings, and reveals the true underlying significance. Rosina has been forced by Carlotta, her step-grandmother, into marriage with Prince Potenziani, but shortly after their marriage, she petitions the Pope for an annulment on the grounds that it has never been consummated. Faced with the prospect of his impotence becoming public knowledge, Potenziani makes a compact with his friend, Prince Nino, to seduce his wife. He does this, but unknown to him, the woman he had seduced is really Agnese della Gherardesci, Rosina's friend. Truth, however, wreaks its revenge. Prince Nino seduces Agnese, and then really falls in love with her; like Jan Bravida with Sabine, he simulates love—and it ends by becoming true. Prince Potenziani, believing that Nino had betrayed him by not carrying out their compact, challenges him to a duel and, in the duel-scene learns the truth from Agnese herself that Nino had really tried to execute their agreement, even though he had failed. Rosina, who all the time has really been in love with her cousin Mario, but has not been allowed to marry him, finally does so, and those who had tried to prevent this are at last forced to acknowledge that they had been in the wrong. All actions in 'The Roads round Pisa' result in consequences which are diametrically opposite to those intended. This ironic pattern of reversal is gradually made clear, and when Carlotta, at the end, sees Rosina's child she herself acknowledges the existence of such a configuration: ' "Life is a mosaic work of the Lord's, which he keeps filling in bit by bit. If I had seen this little bit of bright colour as the centre-piece, I would have understood the pattern and would not have shaken it all to pieces so many times, and given the good Lord so much trouble in putting it together again." '[1]

One person is, however, excluded from this pattern—the main character, Count Augustus, who is unable to find any part in the drama of events played out before him. In this tale the audience of *The Revenge of Truth* is diminished to one spectator, and the fact that he is in no way involved in the central story is just as firmly stressed by the structure.

'The Roads round Pisa' really consists of one story inside another. There is the one, described in Carlotta's words as 'a mosaic', which in turn is composed of a whole series of smaller accounts, marked off in sections, numbered, and given sub-headings: 'III. The Old Lady's Story', 'IV. The Young Lady's Sorrows', 'V. The Story of the Bravo', and so on. These individual pieces all form part of the inner story's design, centering around Prince Nino, Potenziani, Agnese, Rosina and Carlotta—the story in which Augustus is not involved. Around this mosaic there is a kind of frame, composed of references to events which have taken place before the central story opens, and which are communicated to Augustus piece by piece. 'The Roads round Pisa', as a result, develops retrospectively by a series of backward glances, by means of which the current events are set in another perspective for Augustus and, through him, for the reader. This growth of comprehension thus makes up the complete tale within which the central mosaic-design is embedded as a kind of long inset story.

This device of an inset story—or even a whole series of them —is one that Isak Dinesen uses quite frequently, and it has often been likened to the Chinese puzzle where a series of boxes fit inside first one then the other. This is very much more than

[1] *Seven Gothic Tales*, p. 215.

hsimply an ingenious narrative structure, however, since, throug the juxtaposition of the inset story with the whole tale itself, an essential theme is expressed—that of the way in which art is rigorously divorced from the conditions of real life. The significance that the story within the story in 'The Roads round Pisa' acquires by representing this, is one that is also found in several of Isak Dinesen's other tales. In 'The Poet', for example, in which Augustus also appears, the inner story centres upon the love between Anders and Fransine which the Councillor, the main character, tries to turn into a great work of art, and fails, when the forces of life reassert themselves. In 'A Consolatory Tale' Charlie Despard is troubled at the beginning of the story by the relationship between the artist and his public and between art and life. '"What good do we do them?"' he asks his friend, Aeneas Snell, '"What good, in the end, is art to man?"' To answer him Aeneas tells him a tale based on one in the Arabian Nights. In Aeneas's story Fath, the beggar, reveals to the Caliph how rich and poor, man and woman, life and death are, as he says 'two locked caskets, of which each contains the key to the other'. In this Charlie sees a parable of his own situation, the inset story has revealed the significance of art, and he accepts the fact that both art and the artist are sundered from life, and can never be reconciled to it, without losing the separate identity defining both states, and thus endowing each with meaning. In 'The Young Man with the Carnation', the companion-piece in *Winter's Tales* to 'A Consolatory Tale', the structural arrangement is reversed: there, as we have seen, the story of the young man, enclosed within the complete tale, represents life to Charlie, the artist, who is barred from participating in it.

There is no need to elaborate further upon how the major theme is similarly expressed by the form in 'The Immortal Story', where the same structure is adopted of a story within a story, which Mr Clay, the old merchant, tries to turn into life; but one can perhaps remark in passing how strikingly the theme was made apparent through the way in which Orson Welles, in the film he made of the tale, brought the character of Mr Clay to life. Moreover, a remark, that Isak Dinesen made in an interview held in connection with the publication of *Anecdotes of Destiny*, is worth quoting. During this she was questioned about what the reporter saw as the ambiguity of the story's title. And her answer is one that helps to confirm that the narrative structure of these stories is one deliberately designed to embody this theme of the polarity between life and art. '"*In Anecdotes of Destiny* one of the stories is called 'The Immortal Story'. Do you mean by this that the story is immortal?" "Not the story I have written, but the story within the story."'[1]

It is, however, in 'The Roads round Pisa' that this structure is found at its most elaborate and where the implications of the difference between the inset story and the tale become most complex. The major similarity and the major difference between 'The Roads round Pisa' and *The Revenge of Truth* can be isolated if one transposes the tale's narrative structure into terms of the theatre. The audience who watched the marionette comedy is personified in Augustus, but as the sole member of the public he is now no longer sitting in the auditorium: Augustus, in a sense, is moved on to the stage itself, and the drama he sees is one performed on the inner stage, where the action, involving the other characters and culminating in the duel-scene, takes place.

To accentuate Augustus's situation and to show that he stands in marked contrast to the other figures, he is endowed with very human characteristics which come out most clearly in his attitude to the duel between Prince Nino and Potenziani. Prince Nino asks him to be his second, Augustus agrees, but adds that he thinks '"that it would be better to settle such a quarrel, between friends and over a supper table, in a friendly way, and that you cannot have any wish to fight a man so much older than yourself over nothing"'. What is 'nothing' for Augustus is something quite different for Giovanni. Their reason for fighting the duel, Nino tells him, is that '"we want to find out which of us does really stand best with God"', and he praises the qualities of his opponent in terms which make him seem even more remote from life than he has hitherto appeared. '"As to his being old, it is true that he has lived for twice as many years as

[1] *Berlingske Tidende*, 10th October, 1958.

either you or I, but for all that he is in himself a child compared to any of us. It will be as natural to him to live for two hundred years as for us to live sixty. The things that wear us down do not touch him. He is very wonderful."' Augustus's reply to all this is typical: '"What you have said . . . does not seem to me to make your duel more reasonable. Might he not kill you?"'[1]

Agnese wants to hear from him (for her own ulterior reasons) how the challenge to the duel came about, and questions him eagerly about it. Augustus, thinking that 'he might as well tell her, in case there should be an inquest later on', reveals as much as he knows up to that point, and adds that he was quite unable to see how the quarrel could have led to a fight of life and death. When she asks him if it is possible for both adversaries to kill each other simultaneously, 'Augustus thought his young lady to be, for a student of the stars and of philosophy, of a sanguinary turn of mind',[2] but says cautiously that, although he has never heard of such a thing happening, he supposes it is possible. The same human quality is reflected in his attitude to Rosina's baby, which is simply 'the little bit of bright colour' and the centre-piece of the mosaic's design for Carlotta:

> Augustus had never been able to feel anything but fear in the presence of very young children—though they might, he thought, be of some interest as a kind of promise—and he was surprised to realise that the women were all of the opinion that the baby at this stage had reached its very acme of perfection, and that it was a tragic thing that it should ever have to change. This view, that the human race culminates at birth to decline ever after, impressed him as being easier to live up to than his own.[3]

Augustus occupies a central position in the tale since, as well as being the main character, he is also the person through whom we witness the events. And the living qualities his character thus prominently represents within the tale are just those which were lacking in *The Revenge of Truth*. Moreover, Isak Dinesen has succeeded in weaving them into the texture of the story

---

[1] *Seven Gothic Tales*, p. 194.
[2] ibid., p. 196.
[3] ibid., p. 214.

without nullifying them by schematisation. Nevertheless, the contrast these qualities in Augustus draw with the other figures also demonstrates how very far he really is from being involved in their fate.

Why is this so? Why is he denied a role in their marionette play? Augustus's life-like quality is really the direct result of his position in the story: barred from finding a part to play, he drifts purposelessly through life, like the dreamers who appear so often in Isak Dinesen's stories. The particular type of character to which Augustus belongs, drifts just as aimlessly— but for different reasons. The dreamer is so absorbed in his dream, so possessed by it, that real life pales by comparison with its vividness and constitutes merely a passing distraction. Wrapt in a dream-world, he has no aim in life and his roots are bent askew. Augustus's life, however, *is* rooted in the real world, but in this he has no role, and therefore no stability of character, and no sense of personal identity. He is trapped in a self-enclosed circle. Unable to create an identity, seeking the self which continually eludes him like a mirage, he finds it mirrored only in the minds of others and has to accept the reflection for the substance. He remembers, at the beginning of the story, the room of distorting mirrors in the Panoptikon in Copenhagen to which he had been taken as a child, 'and thought how much this was like real life. So your own self, your personality and existence are reflected within the mind of each of the people you meet and live with, into a likeness, a caricature of yourself, which still lives on and pretends to be, in some way, the truth about you.'[1] Augustus never establishes a firm feeling of identity, and his last action in the story is to take a small mirror out of his pocket and to look searchingly in it.

Augustus is receptive rather than assertive, submitting to experience instead of ordering and shaping it, and seeing life only as a spectacle, as a subject for aesthetic contemplation, not as a field for action. He thus represents a type of character who occurs again and again in Isak Dinesen's work. Like Peter in 'Peter and Rosa' before he changes his attitude, like Pilot or the Baron in 'The Dreamers', or Axel Leth in 'The Invincible

[1] *Seven Gothic Tales*, p. 166.

Slave-Owners', and various others characters, major as well as minor, he belongs to the second category of persons described in the passage on pride in *Out of Africa*. Indeterminate figures, taking the colour of their personality, chameleon-like, from their surroundings, lacking any strongly defined character and suffering from a diffusion of self, they are unaware of any purpose or idea in life which God intended to carry through with them. Instead they meekly accept their own identities according to the ideas other people form of them and their stock at the evaluation others place upon it. This is the way Augustus himself is described both in 'The Poet' and in *Out of Africa* where he also appears in an inset anecdote.[1]

The reader is aware of these facts from the very beginning of 'The Roads round Pisa', but they are only driven forcibly home to Augustus by the performance he attends of *The Revenge of Truth*. Everybody will remember the play, the author declares (with her tongue very firmly lodged in her cheek since it had not even been translated into English), and goes on to quote Amiane's speech about the desirability of coming into a marionette comedy. 'This speech seemed to him suddenly to hold a lot of truth. Yes, he thought, if my life were only a marionette comedy in which I had my part and knew it well, then it might be very easy and sweet. . . . If I have now at last, he thought, come into a marionette play, I will not go out of it again.'[2] Like Amiane, he wishes to become part of a work of art by taking up a role; unlike her, he does not succeed. Moreover, since Augustus is representative of life excluded from art, it is not only he who aspires to the conditions of art—so, too, does life itself.

What are the conditions of art which life endeavours to realise, and which the human being seeks to establish in his own life—or should do? What qualities exist in art in which life is lacking? These, it is clear, are closely bound up with one of the basic concerns in Isak Dinesen's work—that of identity. Art establishes a permanent identity through being in possession of an organic unity derived from the fact that, in contradistinction

[1] *Seven Gothic Tales*, p. 380; *Out of Africa*, p. 261.
[2] *Seven Gothic Tales*, p. 199.

to life, the relationship between the parts and the whole is so integral that a total harmony is created, in which form and content, thought and expression, become indissolubly one. These aspects all cohere into an identity which is immediately recognisable and serves to distinguish art from life. Art is thus superior since all its parts are composed into an ordered design through which the meaning is expressed and its autonomy established. Isak Dinesen once expressed this concept in slightly different words, but with a similar meaning: 'People are always asking me what is the significance of this or that in the tales—"What does this symbolise? What does that stand for?" and I always have a difficult time making them believe that I intend everything as it's stated. It would be terrible if the explanation of the work were outside the work itself.'[1]

Nevertheless, in spite of the supreme importance Isak Dinesen attaches to art, this does not turn entirely into the aesthetic doctrine of art for art's sake. 'Life imitates Art far more than Art imitates life,' Oscar Wilde wrote, and we have already noted a certain similarity between this and her ideas. She would agree—up to a point: for this not only establishes the superiority of art for her, but indicates that it can have a function as a kind of model. Whether or not it performs this function, however, must be entirely the choice of the reader. Life can be made to imitate art by striving for a degree of its perfected order and meaning and thus trying to reproduce its organic unity.

There is, however, a profound conflict here, and Isak Dinesen is by no means the only writer who has been aware of it. If art is greater in the meaning and coherence bestowed by its formal order, this also exacts a price. The qualities art displays of harmony and measured proportion can be developed so far, can become so perfected, that they end by eliminating the human element altogether. Similarly, human life itself, by imitating art, can eventually reach a point where it becomes inhuman, becomes, in effect, 'a mosaic work of the Lord's which he keeps filling in bit by bit'—nothing more and nothing less. A brief comparison with another writer who was

[1] *Paris Review*, p. 56.

also sharply, even agonisingly, aware of this conflict will serve to clarify some of the issues at stake with Isak Dinesen.

In Pirandello's *Six Characters in Search of an Author* there is a speech in which the Father of the play within the play says:

> My drama lies entirely in this one thing . . . In my being conscious that each one of us believes himself to be a single person. But it's not true . . . Each one of us is many persons . . . Many persons . . . according to all the possibilities of being that there are within us. . . . With some people we are one person . . . With others we are somebody quite different . . . And all the time we are under the illusion of always being one and the same person for everybody.[1]

The way in which this passage echoes Pellegrina's words to Marcus Cocoza in 'The Dreamers': 'I will not be one person again . . . I will be always many persons from now,' is very striking, but the parallels with Isak Dinesen's work stretch much further. When the Father refers to 'my drama' here, of course, he is not referring to the play as a whole, but to the drama in which he has been caught up as an unwilling participant. There is, in other words, both a similarity between the dramatic structure of Pirandello's work and the narrative structure of several of Isak Dinesen's stories, and a preoccupation with a similar theme expressed through this. Trapped inside this play within a play, he is a character with a fixed and immutable role to play, and it is this fixity of identity he is rebelling against. If Augustus is trying to get into a work of art and thus find an established singleness of identity, the Father is seeking to lose this by breaking out of art into life. He has been made to appear as a lecher to his step-daughter and, as a result, his whole nature has been summed up in this one incident. He is caught in this moment of suspended time, and his step-daughter is, he says, 'trying to attach to me a reality such as I could never have expected I should have to assume for her.'[2] Because of this, he aspires to the condition of life in which he can lose this fixed identity, strip off the mask of lechery

---

[1] Luigi Pirandello: *Six Characters in Search of an Author*, translated by Frederick May, London, 1960, p. 25.
[2] ibid., p. 25.

fastened upon him, and become, no longer only one, but many persons.

He is confined, like the rest of the characters, in a world of unchanging reality: they are all creations of art. Excluded from life, they are pinioned fast in art, and consequently not subject to the same laws of change and mutability which operate in life with all the possibilities for freedom thus offered. (This theme is brought out again in *Tonight We Improvise* where the director, Hinkfuss, declares that a finished work of art is fixed eternally in immutable form, thereby lies at the opposite pole to life, and consequently offers no latitude whatever for improvisation.) The dividing line between art and life is again underscored at the end of *Six Characters in Search of an Author* when the Father tells the Producer that, although reality changes in life and one can thus become many persons in it, the situation in art is a very different matter: 'Ours doesn't change! You see . . . That's the difference between us! Our reality doesn't change . . . It can't change . . . It can never be in any way different from what it is . . . Because it is already fixed . . . Just as it is . . . For ever! For ever it is *this* reality . . . It's terrible! . . . This immutable reality.'[1]

'That's the difference between us': between characters in art and people in real life, between the immutable reality of art and the ever-changing flux of living; for Isak Dinesen on the other hand, this is not something terrible, as we can see if we turn back to 'The Dreamers' for a moment. When Pellegrina decides to be many persons, she has reached the state of freedom that the father in Pirandello's play, trapped in a work of art, longs for, but cannot attain. But this transition from art to the unbounded freedom of life is not one for which Pellegrina strives.[2] On the contrary, she is expelled from art into life by losing her voice, and she has no choice but to comply, nor is

[1] op. cit., p. 58.
[2] The fact that she has made this transition becomes even more apparent in the light of a remark that Isak Dinesen made elsewhere. Pellegrina was a singer. 'Few women,' Isak Dinesen once said, 'have been great artists except in such fields where they do not create a work of art, but can be described as actually *becoming* works of art—i.e. as actors, dancers and singers.' (*Essays*, p. 84.)

there the least doubt which state she prefers. Moreover, she spends the rest of her life trying to recreate the same conditions of art, by donning a mask and playing a role, until she is again forced by circumstances to move on to the next.

Pirandello, nevertheless, has an ambivalent attitude to art. If it can become intolerable by its fixity and immutability, it also, through this immutability, partakes of eternity, and becomes a kind of immortal story removed from the ever-passing moment and flux of life. The Father tells the Producer that:

> He who has the good fortune to be born a living character may snap his fingers at Death even. He will never die! Man . . . The writer . . . The instrument of creation . . . will die . . . But what is created by him will never die. And in order to live eternally he has not the slightest need of extraordinary gifts or of accomplishing prodigies. Who was Sancho Panza? Who was Don Abbondio? And yet they live eternally because—living seeds—they had the good fortune to find a fruitful womb—a fantasy which knew how to raise and nourish them, and to make them live through all eternity.[1]

One finds the same idea expressed in Isak Dinesen's work. In 'The Roads round Pisa' there is a discussion between Monti the poet, and a Monsignor Talbot:

> 'Monti, who had just finished his *Don Giovanni*, had for some time been sunk in a deep melancholy . . . and Monsignor Talbot asked him what was the matter with him . . . So Monti asked him whether he did not think that it might weigh upon a man's mind to have created a human being who was to burn through eternity in hell. Talbot smiled at him and declared that this could only happen to real people. Whereupon the poet cried out and asked him if his Don Giovanni were not real . . . Monsignor Talbot asked him if he did really believe himself a creator in the same sense as God.
>
> '"God!" Monti cried, "God! Do you not know that what God really wants to create is my Don Giovanni, and the Odysseus of Homer, and Cervantes's knight?"[2]

[1] *Six Characters*, pp. 10–11.
[2] *Seven Gothic Tales*, pp. 187–188.

Even in Isak Dinesen, where the balance is tipped much more in favour of art, there is still something of the same ambivalence of attitude. The dual nature of this concept has, of course, been expressed by many other writers. Yeats's Byzantium poems, for instance, treat this theme and one finds the same idea in Keats's odes. It is inherent, for example, in all the ambiguity and conflicting feelings clustering around his description of the Grecian urn as a 'Cold Pastoral'. Isak Dinesen also wrote her 'Grecian Urn'—even if the questions posed are slightly different. What happens when we try to force life to conform entirely to the shape of art and to become, in Yeats's phrase, an 'artifice of eternity?' If art is more harmonious than life, when does this harmony change into discord? What is the result of the attempt to impose an artistic pattern rigidly and inexorably upon life? These are the sort of questions raised—and answered—by some of the stories, by 'The Immortal Story', for example, but pre-eminently by 'The Poet', the story in *Seven Gothic Tales* which forms the counter-balance to 'The Roads round Pisa'.

It takes place in the eighteen-thirties in the small town of Hirschholm (now called Hørsholm) near Rungsted. The history of the town is rapidly sketched in at the beginning of the story and its setting is rendered with all that economy and assurance which are such characteristic features of her descriptions of place—whether of Kenya or of Denmark:

Now the beech forests of the province unfolded themselves. The grey rain fell for a few days around all the world as the veil around a bride, and there came a morning when all the woods were green.

This happens in Denmark every year in May, but impresses you every year, as it impressed these people of a hundred years ago, as something entirely surprising and inexplicable. Through all the long months of winter you have been, even within the deep of the woods, exposed to the winds and the bleak light of heaven. Then, all of a sudden, the month of May builds a dome over your head, and creates for you a refuge, a mysterious sanctuary for all human hearts. The young light foliage, soft as silk, springs out here and there like little tufts of down, little new wings, which the forest is hanging out and trying on. But the next day, or the day after, you walk in a bower . . . Then all the country goes to the woods! to the woods! to make the most of a glory which does not last, for soon the leaves will darken and harden, and a shadow sink within.[1]

Living amidst all this life, the Councillor still has no real place in it; he lives alone, and plays no part in the life of the small town. He is now middle-aged, had been in Weimar during his youth, met Goethe there, and always after had thought of him as a kind of ideal. Art constitutes everything for him, 'outside of poetry there was to him no real ideal in life'. Frustrated by his lack of artistic talents from writing great poetry, he decides to devote himself entirely to turning life into a work of art, and to satisfy his ambitions to be a poet in that way. Using the material at hand, he bends all his energies to creating a great work out of the relationship between Anders Kube, his protegé, and Fransine, a widow, who has recently come to live at Hirschholm. The first meeting of these two was, he thought, 'like the opening bars of a piece of music, or the first chapter of a romance called "Anders and Fransine". Geheimerat Goethe, he reflected, might —would indeed—have made something of it.'[2] Playing with their lives, rearranging them according to his own design, he manipulates these two people through a series of events like puppets in a play. He reads Karl Gutzkow's novel, *Wally: Die Zweiflerin*, and this gives him fresh inspiration. He decides to make the love between Anders and Fransine culminate in a replica of one of its scenes; he stage-manages this, and conceals himself to watch their meeting. At this point the tale reaches its *dénouement*. The forces of flesh and blood assert themselves, Anders steps out of the role in the Councillor's intended work of art, and shoots him. Fatally wounded, he manages to crawl home, there to be confronted by Fransine who has also been awakened to life by her love for Anders. The puppet has now vanished for ever and been replaced by a living woman: 'Her fresh and gentle doll's face was dissolved and ruined by tears; the doll had been broken.' Lying in his blood, the Councillor stammers out his final statement of belief in the supremacy of

---

[1] *Seven Gothic Tales*, pp. 378–379.
[2] ibid., p. 370.

art, but Fransine will not hear him: 'He meant to tell her that
the world was good and beautiful, but indeed she knew better . . .
that was the world in which they meant to hang Anders.'[1] A
part of this world at last, she takes the only step left to her and,
picking up a stone, she kills the poet who had brought destruc-
tion upon them.

But before this happens, Count Augustus has been introduced
into the story with the intention of offering a contrast to the
Councillor. He pays him a visit and this also marks a fresh
development in 'The Poet'. If Augustus contemplates life
aesthetically, the Councillor's aestheticism goes much further
and degenerates into a supreme indifference to human life and
suffering. Life for him is only the raw material from which art
can be shaped. He plans to cause a new twist in the situation by
proposing to marry Fransine, and to watch the effect of this
upon Anders. As a result, although unaware of the full consequences this will ultimately have, he himself comes to play an
active part both in the 'inner' story of Anders and Fransine and
in the whole tale. At the end he becomes the poet of the story's
title, dying in a work of his own composition: 'Suddenly the old
Councillor understood everything in the world . . . He had got
inside the magic circle of poetry . . . He might be anything
without ever running any risk, for whatever he did the
author would see to it that things would somehow come out
all right, that high and divine law and order would be maintained.'[2]

Even while Isak Dinesen asserts the strength of life through
Fransine and Anders and shows how, in the end, they refuse to
be constricted within the mould of art, the Councillor himself, at
the moment of death, sees the meaning of all things in a vision—
of art. 'He understood everything in the world': life becomes
entirely and definitively like a work of art—at the point of death.
A note jotted down amongst Isak Dinesen's manuscripts
develops the concept and reveals where it leads to; 'on seeing
life as a whole . . . in the way one sees, as soon as a person dies,
his entire life as a whole, so that the particular circumstances of

[1] *Seven Gothic Tales*, pp. 419–420.
[2] ibid., pp. 415–416.

the moment do not affect one deeply, *but become integrated as only one element in the total picture*.[1]

This indicates the dilemma of this whole theme in Isak Dinesen's work, the genesis of which can be traced back to the nature of her aesthetic concepts. The more the emphasis is placed upon ordering all the components into an aesthetic design—'a total picture', the less like life art becomes and the more inhuman, so that eventually one is 'not affected deeply'. And the logical end of this, the point where the process reaches its culmination, is death itself. On the other hand, the closer art approximates to the conditions of life, the less perfect, in her terms, it becomes. The difficulty, the crucial difficulty, confronting her as a writer (and a person) was to find and maintain a precarious point of balance. There can, I think, be no doubt that she struck this equilibrium in *Out of Africa*—supported by the very nature of that work. Because it is directly based upon autobiographical experience she was not able to transmute it completely into a work of art—in her meaning of the term. And it is here that one can see the limitations of this. One remembers her description of a story when she drew a pentagram, and remarked that likewise there was nothing to add or subtract to a story when it was entirely finished and the meaning stood out clearly defined. In *Out of Africa* she struggles to comprehend the meaning of her diverse experiences, to define them clearly, and succeeds in reconciling them into a philosophy of life. She asks for a sign towards the end of her stay in Kenya, which will explain the meaning underlying all the tribulation she is experiencing, and describes how she sees a cock pluck the tongue out of a chameleon, that has been standing its ground and defying it. In the incident she hears the laughter that reminds her of Job: 'Great powers had laughed to me, with an echo from the hills to follow the laughter, they had said among the trumpets, among the cocks and Chameleons, Ha ha!'[2] But she cannot assimilate her experiences into a theory of art by imposing a finished pattern upon them—inevitably, since her own life's story, unlike that of the man's in the anecdote of the stork, has

[1] My emphasis.
[2] *Out of Africa*, p. 370.

not yet run its full course. These two anecdotes, in fact, represent the diverging tendencies in the book, and it is a divergence that is also mirrored in the much looser construction of *Out of Africa*. Nor do the persons, drawn from life, fit completely into an overall design, as they are made to in the stories: they vibrate with life in the tension between what they were in reality and the idea she formed of them. Denys Finch-Hatton, for instance, may have seemed to her like an ideal embodiment of a courtier from an early and more gracious period of English history, but he is also very much more in the book. He is not boxed up inside the pentagram of art, and the same is true of the other persons— and indeed of the whole of *Out of Africa*.

Whether the same balance between the conditions represented by art and life is maintained in the stories like 'The Roads round Pisa' or 'The Poet', where Isak Dinesen is directly concerned with these concepts, is doubtful. These are really literary artefacts about the lack of relation between artefact and reality, art and life, even if, in a wider sense, they do form a part of life, since they augment reality by creating something previously non-existent. They are indeed formally beautiful in their intricate design and finished and rounded perfection, neverthe-less, when people and their experiences are valued more as com-ponent parts of a design than as human beings, when life is sacrificed to an aesthetic programme, then a reduction in human value inevitably follows.

A critic who welcomes this dissociation and applauds its consequences is Ortega y Gasset in his essay 'The Dehumaniza-tion of Art'—an essay in aesthetic theory which has much relevance to this aspect of Isak Dinesen's work. Starting from the premise that 'tears and laughter are, aesthetically, frauds', Ortega holds that 'not only is grieving and rejoicing at such human destinies as a work of art presents or narrates a very different thing from true aesthetic pleasure, but preoccupation with the human content of the work is in principle incompatible with aesthetic enjoyment proper'.[1] He concludes that, as a consequence:

[1] *The Dehumanization of Art*, p. 9.

Even though pure art may be impossible there doubtless can prevail a tendency towards a purification of art. Such a tendency would effect a progressive elimination of the human, all too human, elements predominant in romantic and naturalistic production. And in this process a point can be reached in which the human content has grown so thin that it is negligible. We then have an art which can be comprehended only by people possessed of the peculiar gift of artistic sensibility—an art for artists and not for the masses, for 'quality' and not for hoi polloi.[1]

This is indeed to purify art with a vengeance, but the question whether Isak Dinesen's writing ever reaches the point of 'pure art', where the human content becomes completely negligible, is an open one. Possibly in some of her tales it comes perilously close; in others, like 'Sorrow-Acre', for example, or 'Copenhagen Season', it falls far short. Moreover, the play of her wit, such a pronounced feature of her work, which enlivens it with such sparkle and grace, must also be taken into account. Of one thing, however, there can be no doubt. She does succeed in illustrating the difficulty of the task which she set herself in conformity with her conception of life and art, and in demonstrating the rigorous severity of the response she requires from the reader.

[1] *The Dehumanization of Art,* p. 11.

146

8

Acting and the Mask of Comedy

'I do often intend a comic sense, I love a joke, I love the humorous,' Isak Dinesen once said,[1] and she does intend a comic sense with her stories—even though the comedy is frequently rather an austere one. Obviously there are major exceptions to this. 'The Monkey', for instance, is grotesquely comic and wonderfully funny. Boris, a young lieutenant in the Royal Guards, has become involved in a scandal with a circle of friends, and to avert disgrace, needs to get married as soon as possible, as a sign of respectable normality. He visits his aunt, the prioress of Closter Seven, a lay-convent, wealthily endowed as an establishment for elderly ladies belonging to the nobility (like some still in existence in Denmark). News of his threatened disgrace has already reached the secluded convent ahead of him:

> The ladies had not discussed these happenings much amongst themselves, but the librarian of the convent, who was a theologian and a scholar, had been dragged away into more than one *tête-à-tête*, and encouraged to give his opinion on the problem. From him they had learnt to connect it somehow with those romantic and sacred shores of ancient Greece which they had till now held in high esteem. Remembering their young days, when everything Greek had been *le dernier cri*, and frocks and coiffures had been named *à la grecque*, they wondered—Could the expression be used also to designate anything so little related to their young ladies' dreams of refinement? They had loved those frocks, they had waltzed with princes in them; now they thought of them with uneasiness.[2]

[1] *Paris Review*, p. 56.
[2] *Seven Gothic Tales*, pp. 111–112.

The prioress decides that the only way out is for Boris to marry the highly aristocratic Athena Hopballehus, 'a strong young woman of eighteen, six feet high and broad in proportion, with a pair of shoulders which could lift and carry a sack of wheat'. When Boris goes to see her to make his proposal of marriage, 'safe in her great strength, she asked him—standing, as was her habit, on one leg, like a big stork—of news of his aunt'.[1] The supremely baroque touch could hardly be bettered. She decides to refuse the offer, and her father writes to Boris to tell him of her decision. Boris's aunt is infuriated that her plans should be crossed in this way:

'And all that you have offered her—the position, the influence, the future—that means nothing to her? What is it she wants to be?' She looked into the letter, but in her agony she was holding it, bewildered, upside down. 'A stone figure upon a sarcophagus— in the dark, in silence, forever? Here we have a fanatical virgin, *en plein dixneuvième siècle? Vraiment tu n'as pas de la chance!* There is no *horror vaccui* here.'

'The law of the *horror vaccui*,' Boris, who was really frightened, said to distract her, 'does not hold good more than thirty-two feet up.'

'More than what?' asked the Prioress.

'Thirty-two feet,' he said. The Prioress shrugged her shoulders.[2]

They plan that Boris should seduce her one night and thus compel her into marriage. After he has struggled mightily to do so, and failed, because Athena is the stronger, they make a last attempt to force her to comply with their plans. The next morning his aunt suggests that Athena may be with child:

Athena's world was evidently tumbling down to the right and left of her, like a position under heavy gunfire, but still she stood up straight. 'What?' she asked. 'Shall I have a child from that?'

The old woman looked hard at her. 'Athena,' she said after a moment . . . 'the last thing I wish is to destroy what innocence you may still have left. But it is more than likely that you will have a child.'

---

[1] *Seven Gothic Tales*, pp. 129–130.
[2] ibid., p. 137.

'If I have a child,' said Athena, from her quaking earth thrusting at the heavens, 'my father will teach him astronomy.'[1]

'Babette's Feast' is a tale which has a warm, infectious humour. When Babette, the former French communard, comes as a cook to the two maiden sisters living frugally in a small provincial town in Norway, they do not really believe that she can cook. 'In France they knew that people ate frogs. They showed Babette how to prepare a split cod and an ale-and-bread-soup. during the demonstration the Frenchwoman's face became absolutely expressionless.'[2] The tale reaches its climax in the richly comic scene where the small, strictly ascetic, religious community eat Babette's splendid feast in the same spirit of self-abnegation which they bring to everything.

Comedy in a vein totally different from the extravagantly grotesque is also found in Isak Dinesen: a more devious comedy, and more muted in tone—one of understatement. In *Shadows on the Grass* she describes how one day, going through the farm accounts, she discovered that a 100-rupee note was missing and must have been stolen. She told Farah, who 'very calmly' declared that he would get the money back:

> He walked away, and towards evening returned carrying with him a human skull. This may sound highly dramatic, but was in itself nothing out of the normal. For centuries the Natives had not buried their dead but had laid them out on the plain where jackals and vultures would take care of them . . . Farah rammed down a pole outside my door and nailed the skull to the top of it. I stood by and watched him without enthusiasm.[3]

She adds that this worked, however, despite her lack of enthusiasm: next morning the missing note was found at the foot of the pole.

In *Shadows on the Grass* she also relates how she had been ordered by the doctor to take six drops of arsenic after meals in a glass of water. One evening, Abdullai, a boy in the house,

---

[1] *Seven Gothic Tales*, p. 158
[2] *Anecdotes of Destiny*, p. 36.
[3] op. cit., p. 27.

brought her the medicine while she was sitting reading after dinner, she swallowed it abstractedly, and immediately after realised that it must have contained pure arsenic. She asked Abdullai and he confirmed this:

> 'Then I think that I shall die, Abdullai,' I said, 'and you must send Farah in to me.' Later on Farah told me that his little brother had come rushing into his house, and cried out: 'I have killed Memsahib! Go in to her, you! And goodbye to you all, for I am going away and am never coming back,' and with these words had vanished. By the time when Farah came, I myself had really begun to believe that I was going to die.

She knew of no ways of treating arsenic poisoning, but came to think that this was mentioned in Dumas' novel, *La Reine Margot*:

> I had Farah find Queen Margot on my book-shelf, managed to look up the cure of milk and white-of-egg used, and started upon it, Farah lifting up my head so that I might swallow the medicine. In the midst of the treatment I remembered having been told that great quantities of arsenic will turn the patient a livid blue—in case it was really so, I reasoned, it was hardly worth struggling for life, so I sent for Kamante and had him stand by the bed, from time to time holding up my mirror to me. About midnight I began to think that I might after all remain alive, and about dawn to wonder how we were to get Abdullai back.[1]

This comedy of understatement joins hands with another characteristic Isak Dinesen trait. She knew pre-eminently the virtues of leaving the important things unsaid. Would it not be awful, asks Pierrot in 'Carnival', if people who rely entirely upon God are really doing the very thing which most displeases him. '"Yes," says the other: '"but even if it is so, it cannot matter to us, because we do not believe in God." Pierrot nodded. "No," she said.'' There are also scenes of pure comedy in many of the other stories, nor must one overlook the glints of sparkling wit which flash out again and again in even the most sombre of them, but they light up the darker tone only momentarily, and seldom completely dispel it. Comedy, in the sense of

[1] op. cit., pp. 125–126.

broad humour, in fact, is not the predominant impression one is left with after reading Isak Dinesen's stories. Nevertheless there is another, and more fundamental way, in which they do reveal an idea of comedy.

'If . . . I had my part and knew it well,' Augustus thinks when he sees the marionette comedy in 'The Roads round Pisa', 'then it might be very easy and sweet,' and he notes the theatrical quality which the lives of people in the south of Europe seem to have. 'They were as immune to the terrors, the crimes and the miracles of the life in which they took part as were the little actors upon the old player's stage . . . these people spoke fluently under the wildest passions, as if life were, in any of her whims, a comedy which they had already rehearsed.'[1] By playing a role one is not only fulfilling one's own aspirations, and carrying out the author's (or God's) intentions; one can also conduct one's life with the complete confidence of an actor working from a script, in which has been written what has happened in the past, the meaning of what is going on at the present, and with the answer to what is to come in one's hands. Under these conditions life does become a comedy 'already rehearsed'.

But even if many of Isak Dinesen's characters take part in a comedy, and wear motley, the jest of fate is often one made at their expense. There is no certainty—as she herself discovered only too well—that the playwright is benevolently disposed. The all-powerful God of Isak Dinesen is much more that of the Old Testament than of the New—a jealous, even vengeful Jehovah, visiting the characters' sins of omission upon their own heads. The revenge executed on those who do not follow the author's general plan is as remorselessly carried out and has all the inexorable quality that, as a young woman, she had encountered in her lessons in perspective drawing. If properly carried out, the result was bound to be correct, but if there were any negligence, 'then vengeance would be wreaked at the end of the problem, invariably, and with a terrible force'. There is, in fact, 'an inflexible justice' (to use her own words about perspective drawing again) about this view of life. Those persons who

[1] *Seven Gothic Tales,* p. 199.

have made the irrevocable choice of participating in this play-acting must carry this through regardless of the cost. If they attempt to depart from their role then they are punished according to their deserts by being forced back into true perspective. They become marionettes, like Mr Clay in 'The Immortal Story', who, sitting slumped in his chair at the end, 'looked like a jumping-jack when the hand which has pulled the strings has suddenly let them go.' Like Potenziani and Prince Nino they are delivered into stronger hands than their own, and are helplessly jerked into their true place, and back to their proper role by the all-powerful puppet-master. The intention is deliberate, as Isak Dinesen acknowledged: 'To depict how such characters as Potenziani and Prince Nino are punished according to their deserts, one by death, the other with remorse and despair, is a part of the action of the story.'[1] They become part of a divine comedy (Prince Nino and Agnese actually resolve their entanglement by quoting passages from Dante), but it is one more divine than comic in the usual sense of the world. The mirth these characters arouse is the same as Karen Blixen herself heard when she saw the cock pluck out the chameleon's tongue, and great powers had laughed to her—or at her.

This conception of comedy and the attitude it calls forth are epitomised in the final scene between Kasparson and Miss Malin in the tale, 'The Deluge at Norderney':

> 'Well,' said Miss Malin after a pause, 'and did you enjoy playing the role of the Cardinal when you had your chance at last? Did you have a pleasant time?'
>
> 'As God liveth, Madame, I had that,' said Kasparson, 'a good night and day. For I have lived long enough, by now, to have learned, when the devil grins at me, to grin back. And what now if this—to grin back when the devil grins at you—be in reality the highest, the only true fun in all the world?'[2]

Comedy is a means of steeling oneself heroically to endure; it is really a mask which conceals the sentient human being from the public gaze.

[1] From a letter of Isak Dinesen's quoted in Hans Brix's *Analyser og Problemer*, Vol. VI, Copenhagen, 1950, p. 300.
[2] *Seven Gothic Tales*, pp. 77–78.

Kasparson has a double role in this story: he is both the actor, Kasparson, and he plays the part of the Cardinal. This duality of role is something typical for many of the figures in Isak Dinesen's stories; in effect, it constitutes her main method of characterisation. The significance of this method and the way it springs from a central idea in her work can be seen if we turn from the tales to the figure of Old Knudsen in *Out of Africa*:

> He never spoke of himself except in the third person, as 'Old Knudsen', and never without boasting and bragging to the last degree. There was not a thing in the world that Old Knudsen would not undertake and carry through, and not a champion fighter whom Old Knudsen could not knock down ... The great exploits and achievements of Old Knudsen and his eminence in everything, as he reported these things to me, were clearly at variance with the weakness and impotency of the old man who reported them; in the end you felt that you were dealing with two separate and essentially different individualities. The mighty figure of Old Knudsen rose in the background, unbeaten and triumphant, the hero of all the adventures, and it was his old bent and worn servant whom I knew, and who never tired of telling me about him. This little, humble man had made it his mission in life to uphold and extol the name of Old Knudsen, even to death. For he had really seen Old Knudsen, which nobody else except God ever had, and after that he would stand no heresy in anyone.[1]

The myth of 'Old Knudsen' is the idea that God had when he created him and which Knudsen himself whole-heartedly believes in and devoutly serves. In contrast to this legendary figure, there is the actual reality of the worn-out old man; the discrepancy between the two is so great that he is also aware of this, and speaks of himself only in the third person. One thinks of Pellegrina doing precisely the same, and devoting her life to ensuring that the Pellegrina Leoni legend should remain untouched by reality. The old man has really the soul of an artist; he applies his imagination to his own life, and shapes the raw material into a deliberate artistic composition. Drawn from life, depicted in Karen Blixen's autobiographical record, Knudsen

[1] *Out of Africa*, pp. 58–59.

is well over half-way to becoming a typical Isak Dinesen character.

But even though his life is an act staged between the actual man and a role he assumes, we do, nevertheless, see the real person very clearly. In the stories, however, the human being is relegated to the wings, while the role he is playing occupies the centre of the stage. The nature of some of these roles is even indicated by the titles of some of the stories: 'The Old Chevalier', 'The Poet', 'The Invincible Slave-Owners', 'The Heroine', 'The Caryatides'; all show the parts which the main characters assume. In others, the bold outline of their act is rapidly sketched in. Jensine in 'The Pearls' performs the part of a fearless, young woman; Alkmene, in the story with that title, acts that of a prudent, pious one—and both their acts are really masks which conceal the true nature of the person wearing them. Kasparson plays the part of the Cardinal, Pellegrina plays many parts, and the old lord in 'Sorrow-Acre' plays only one.

The way in which, in the stories, the real person moves into the background can be illustrated by 'The Supper at Elsinore'. The reader is made to realise the emptiness and the futility of the existence of those who, like Augustus, do not act in life, even if the theme, which in much of Isak Dinesen's work is either tragic, or potentially so, is here treated with a distinct tinge of irony, which both turns the story into a tragi-comic one and again effectively distances it. As with Augustus in 'The Roads round Pisa', Isak Dinesen uses the metaphor of a mirror to depict the lives of the two young De Coninck sisters:

> . . . they stood in a strange, distorted relation to the world, as if it had been only their reflection in a mirror which they had been showing it, while in the background and the shadow the real woman remained a looker-on. . . . Perhaps the lovely sisters derived a queer pleasure out of the adoration paid to their images in the mirror. They could not do without it in the end.[1]

Images reflected in a mirror, they live only in a looking-glass world, and we are made further aware of this by the contrast

[1] *Seven Gothic Tales*, p. 220.

between their lives and that of the period in which the story is set.

It opens in Denmark during the times of the Napoleonic wars. After the bombardment of Copenhagen by the British navy, a fleet of privateers is established, and the whole Danish nation follows the exploits of these with pride and admiration. Morten De Coninck commands a privateer and plays a major part in all the glory and heroism of the times. When the war is over, however, instead of marrying and settling down in Elsinore, he leaves quite suddenly, and never returns. His two sisters hear news of him from time to time and invest his life with all the glamour and the heroism in which their own is so notably lacking. 'To Morten's sisters the infrequent news of their brother was manna on which they kept their hearts alive in a desert. . . . Their brother would come back an admiral in a foreign fleet, his breast covered with unknown stars, to marry the bride waiting for him, or come back wounded, broken in health, but highly honoured, to die in Elsinore.'[1] They live in these romantic dreams, even though Morten's fate is really something very different: he had gone to the West Indies, resumed his privateering, and had eventually been captured and hanged for piracy.

The two sisters live on and become old maids. One evening their old housekeeper comes to Copenhagen from their child-hood home in Elsinore and tells them that she has seen Morten's ghost several times in the house. The two sisters go there to meet him. The supernatural element in the story is treated with a demurely mischievous humour which does not altogether con-ceal the fact that it has a sharp edge. Why have they never, they wonder, been back in their old home before? 'Was it that the house of their childhood and young days had seemed to them a little empty and cold, a little grave-like, until it had a ghost in it?'[2] Morten tells them that he has come straight from hell, and describes the exploits of his former life as a pirate. 'They listened . . . But they were longing to do more . . . Could they not touch him? No, they knew that to be out of the question.

[1] *Seven Gothic Tales*, p. 229.
[2] ibid., p. 251.

They had not been reading ghost stories all their lives for nothing.'[1]

It is in this conversation that they realise the utter emptiness of their own existence, and where the tragi-comedy becomes most pronounced. At the end the elder sister cries:

> 'Yes, . . . you may talk. But you mean to go away again and leave me. You! You have been to these great warm seas of which you talk, to a hundred countries. You have been married to five people —Oh, I do not know of it all! It is easy for you to speak quietly, to sit still. You have never needed to beat your arms to keep warm. You do not need to now!'
> Her voice failed her . . . 'And here,' she groaned out, 'I am— cold. The world is bitterly cold around me. I am so cold at night, in my bed, that my warming-pans are no good to me!'

The clock strikes midnight and it is time for Morten to return to hell:

> Fanny meant to go on speaking, and to lift at last all the deadly weight of her whole life off her . . . She could not out-talk the clock . . .
> 'Oh, hell,' she cried out, 'to hell!' . . .
> 'Morten!' she cried in a long wail. 'Brother! Stay! Listen! Take me with you!'[2]

The two sisters have invested all their hopes and dreams in their brother. Morten is the embodiment of these dreams, their *alter ego*. He had lived a life full of adventure and action; they have been mere spectators; and finally the real women come to life—as ghosts.

There is another sense in which acting is of considerable importance in Isak Dinesen. The theatrical element in Karen Blixen's own life has previously been noted, and her tales are full of references to the theatre. Many of her characters are either actors by profession or connected in some way with the stage. Pino Pizzuti, for example, in 'Night Walk', 'Of Hidden Thoughts and of Heaven', and the unpublished 'Second Meeting', is the director of a marionette theatre; Herr Soerensen in

---

[1] *Seven Gothic Tales*, p. 254.
[2] ibid., pp. 268–269.

'Tempests' is also a theatre director. Kasparson in 'The Deluge at Norderney' has been an actor; Malli in 'Tempests' is an actress, and this both influences her life and is a main factor in the tale; Pellegrina Leoni has been an opera-singer, continues her act in life, and dies playing the part of Donna Anna in *Don Giovanni*; Heloise, the main character in 'The Heroine', is a music-hall dancer, and her profession has a vital bearing upon the story. Each of these characters is only the particular embodiment of a general concept.

Implicit in her tales—at times, made explicit—is a concept of the character as an actor and of his life as a game of play-acting. In 'The Monkey', Boris is described as being:

> ... not dogmatic enough to believe that you must have boards and footlights to be within the theatre; he carried the stage with him in his heart. ... To him the theatre was real life. As long as he could not act, he was puzzled by the world and uncertain what to do with it; but as an actor he was his true self, and as soon as he could see a situation in the light of the theatre, he would feel at home in it.[1]

'To him the theatre was real life . . . as an actor he was in true self': the actor in fact reveals himself by pretending to be someone else. The histrionic possibilities are very considerable, and Isak Dinesen exploits them to the full.

In those stories where the figures (in contrast to the De Coninck sisters) do find a part to play, the attitude they take to this is the crucial factor which determines their characterisation. Kasparson, Pellegrina Leoni as an opera-singer, the Cardinal, Malli, the old lord in 'Sorrow-Acre', Heloise in 'The Heroine', the Councillor, while he is acting as a poet, and many others— each responds to a situation theatrically. Drawn larger than life, they strike a pose, and compose their actions and their speech into a rhetorical stance. Isak Dinesen does not so much portray a character, as design a role, and instead of depicting an individual character, she describes the traits of an actor. The formal, elaborate qualities of her dialogue originate partly from the fact

---

[1] *Seven Gothic Tales*, pp. 140–141.

that it is written for an actor to declaim deliberately and self-consciously. The attention of her characters is fixed upon no one so much as upon themselves, and they are chiefly engaged in pondering aloud upon the significance of their parts. And if Karen Blixen herself combined several different figures in one and the same person, Isak Dinesen's characters combine two main ones. They are really, like Old Knudsen, two persons in one, actor and audience, person and role. They constitute their own best and most appreciative audience, weighing every gesture critically, appraising every *coup de theatre*. At the end of 'The Deluge at Norderney', Kasparson strips away his mask, steps forward as the real man, and judiciously assesses the quality of his performance:

'I am an actor. Shall not an actor have a role? ... The proof of our undertaking is in the success or fiasco. I have played the part well. The Cardinal would have applauded me, for he was a fine connoisseur of the art ...' 'The only thing,' he went on after a pause, 'which he might have criticized is this: he might have held that I overdid my role. I stayed in this hayloft to save the lives of those sottish peasants, who preferred the salvation of their cattle to their own. It is doubtful whether the Cardinal would ever have done that, for he was a man of excellent sense. That may be so. But a little charlatanry there must needs be in all great art, and the Cardinal himself was not free from it.'[1]

It is this concept of the person's other self as an actor staging a performance which determines Isak Dinesen's method of characterisation. It follows the same lines traced out by the stories: these are not realistic, and neither is the characterisation a psychologically-orientated realistic one. And this is so, despite the fact that many of her characters are really split personalities —but not split in a psychological sense. If her characters do have a kind of introspective quality, the analysis they conduct is of their acting procedures much more than it is an exploration of their processes of thought. And this analysis is carried on in two ways: through self-consciously formulated dialogue, and through the way they give physical expression to their inner

[1] *Seven Gothic Tales*, pp. 74–75.

thoughts and feelings. They both say and act what they think and feel. This portrayal of the internal reactions through external display is, of course, a traditional method with writers who are not mainly concerned with the inner life—Fielding's characters offer frequent examples of the same technique—but with Isak Dinesen, the stage-effects are even more pronounced. Her characters are actors rendering their inner life by theatrically stylised gestures, exaggerating them, to ensure that their effect will carry well beyond the footlights. They change colour vividly, they grow rigid with rage or terror, they shake with laughter, they tremble with anger, fear or grief, above all—Isak Dinesen's favourite expression—they give a *great* glance. They also blush—in all hues of red. She established a whole story, *Ehrengard*, around the desire of Herr Cazotte, an artist, to call forth a blush in the woman of his choice. His reasons for wishing to make Ehrengard do this are set out in one of his letters:

> What will be now, to the true artist, the *fine fleur* of her being? In what act is a nature like hers, within the chosen moment, to give itself forth most exhaustively? I have pictured her in every possible situation and posture, in itself a sweet pursuit. And I made my decision. *In the blush* . . . What is really to happen to this admirable, this unique nature is to happen within herself.[1]

At the end of the story, however, it is he who is forced to blush—at considerable length, and most expressively. 'Herr Cazotte's blood was drawn upwards, as from the profoundest wells of his being, till it coloured him all over like a transparent crimson veil. His brow and cheeks, all on their own, radiated a divine fire, a celestial, deep-rose flame, as if they were giving away a long-kept secret.'

The dramatic feature in Isak Dinesen's tales is one that is inherent in this central relationship that exists between a character's consciousness of his mask and the mask, or role, itself. The role, that the characters play, delineates the main features of their mask; this becomes the explicit theme of 'The Deluge at Norderney'. 'Let it be the hour of the falling of the

---

[1] *Ehrengard*, New York, 1963, pp. 35–36.

mask . . . tell me who you are,'[1] the 'Cardinal' says to the other characters marooned with him in the hay-loft. Miss Malin, an elderly maiden lady, has donned a mask in life, one with the lineaments of profligacy and sensuality etched upon it. She was, we are told, a little mad, and her madness assumed 'the curious form of a firm faith in a past of colossal licentiousness . . . she could not open her mouth without referring to her days of debauchery . . . In all her fantasies she was her own heroine.'[2] Kasparson and Miss Malin are the two main persons; the other two also wear a mask—with a difference.

Jonathan Mærsk had created a successful career for himself as a singer amongst fashionable society in Copenhagen. Eventually, however, a friend reveals the truth that Jonathan is really the illegitimate son of one of the most influential men in society at the time. His audience had known this, and what he had taken to be the plaudits of his talents were really derived, his friend tells him, from the fact that: 'they have been watching you all the time to see if the soul of Baron Gersdorff was showing itself in you, in which case you would be the richest man, and the best match . . . in all northern Europe'.[3] Unable to divest himself, whatever he does, of this *persona*, he becomes completely misanthropic, and finally leaves Copenhagen. Calypso, the remaining character in the quartet that composes 'The Deluge at Norderney', had been brought up by her uncle, who is homosexual. He at first tries to mask the fact that she is a girl by dressing her in boy's clothing, then finally ignores her presence completely, when she is no longer able to disguise her true sex. At last Calypso realizes that she has a life and personality of her own as a girl, and flees from her uncle's castle.

Both of these characters have had a *persona* imposed upon them by others. They thus represent an intermediate stage between the two types of persons described in the passage on pride in *Out of Africa*. They refuse 'to accept as success what others warrant to be so', and reject the *personae* other people have tried to force upon them. Kasparson had also been assigned

---

[1] *Seven Gothic Tales*, p. 27.
[2] ibid., pp. 21–22.
[3] ibid., p. 33.

a role by others: that of the Cardinal's valet. And he too rejects this. When his opportunity comes during the floods, he seizes his opportunity to change from a mere understudy to the star role, murders his master, and plays the part of the Cardinal, because, as he says, 'not by the face shall the man be known, but by the mask'.

Kasparson is a typical Isak Dinesen figure in another way, one which not only leads back to Old Knudsen and the dual role he plays, but also points to the way in which the idea behind his conception is a central one. It was very seldom that Isak Dinesen commented upon her stories, but Aage Henriksen quotes a remark which she once made about 'The Deluge at Norderney'; "'I suppose you have understood," she said, "that the two figures, the Cardinal and Kasparson, are really one and the same person." [1] The relationship between these two is not only that of master and servant; the Cardinal is also Kasparson's *alter ego*, dispatched into the wings by Kasparson killing him off-stage, on his way into the limelight. Their relationship is like that of Pellegrina to her various identities, or that between Pizzuti and Byron in 'Second Meeting'. Kasparson in fact becomes the quintessential artist, setting the scene, directing the characters, stage-managing the performance and, in the process, transmuting his life into a legendary work of art. To achieve this, he sacrifices the Cardinal's life—his 'real' self. But which one *is* real? The man dies, and yet from his death, the artist is born—wearing a mask. It is in this paradox that Isak Dinesen's whole concept of the mask and of acting is rooted.

[1] *Det guddommelige Barn*, p. 99.

9

Attitude to God

During the great flood at Norderney the 'Cardinal' (in reality, Kasparson) plays such a vital part in all the rescue-work that ever afterwards it was known as 'the flood of the Cardinal'. 'This was because in the midst of their misery the terror-stricken people got support from one already half-mythical figure, and felt at their side the presence of a guardian angel. Many years after, in the minds of the peasants, it seemed that his company in their dark despair had shed a great white light over the black waves.' So greatly was he venerated that 'after the flood it was said by many that he had been seen to walk upon the waves'.[1] After the rescuers have toiled throughout the day, it is believed by nightfall that they have saved everybody, but then news is brought that there are still some people cut off. The boatmen, exhausted and fearful of the danger, are on the point of refusing to go back, but the 'Cardinal' still displays an unflagging spirit, and orders them to return with him. 'As he walked down to the boat . . . some of the ladies suddenly and wildly clapped their hands. They meant no harm. Knowing heroism only from the stage, they gave it the stage's applause. But the old man whom they applauded stopped under it for a moment. He bowed his head a little, with an exquisite irony, in the manner of a hero upon the stage.'[2] The climax of his act comes a little later. When the boat is returning, it passes a hay-loft in which a peasant-family are stranded with no chance of being saved until the following day; there is not enough room in the boat for them all, but the 'Cardinal', true to the Christ-like

[1] *Seven Gothic Tales*, pp. 4–7.
[2] ibid., pp. 8–9.

spirit which has apparently imbued him the whole time, offers to sacrifice himself by remaining in their stead. Miss Malin and the two young people follow his example, the family replaces them in the boat, and the 'Cardinal' and the other three are left alone to await rescue—and to let the mask fall.

There are, however, for Isak Dinesen, more ways than one of acting like Christ. '"Where in all the world,"' Miss Malin asks the 'Cardinal', '"did you get the idea that the Lord wants the truth from us?"'

'It is a strange, a most original, idea of yours, My Lord. Why, he knows it already, and may even have found it a little bit dull . . . I, on the contrary, have always held that the Lord has a penchant for masquerades . . . The Lord himself—with your permission— seems to me to have been masquerading pretty freely at the time when he took on flesh and dwelt amongst us . . .' 'Indeed, My Lord,' she went on, 'of all monarchs of whom I have ever heard, the one who came, to my mind, nearest to the true spirit of God was the Caliph Haroun of Baghdad, who as you know, had a taste for disguise.'[1]

Miss Malin, had she known it at the time, need not have looked so far as the Arabian Nights for confirmation of her belief; she had an example much closer at hand of someone who had come 'nearest to the true spirit of God'. By taking over the Cardinal's role Kasparson has created an immortal and divine legend amongst the peasants: after he has let the mask fall, he tells Miss Malin that 'they have seen the face of God in my face'.

In reality, however, they have seen the features of God, not in Kasparson's face—but in his mask; just as, according to Miss Malin, when Christ masqueraded as a human being, mankind saw the face of immortal God in the mask of the mortal man. Kasparson has played the part of God in a double sense. At the end of the story, as dawn breaks, the hay-loft, with its four inmates, is on the point of plunging down into the surrounding flood-waters. Kasparson has made the supreme sacrifice by laying down his own life in order that the peasants might be

[1] *Seven Gothic Tales*, pp. 24–25.

saved (even if previously, during the evening, he had criticised this as overdoing his role). But in an even more vital sense he has also played God—by playing a part. It is not only Karen Blixen who assumed a mask in her own life, not only Isak Dinesen's characters who do this; God Himself did the same. Since, however, Christ was not a man but really God, then the sacrifice He made of His life in order to redeem mankind was really no sacrifice at all. Seen in these terms, the Crucifixion and the Resurrection become really only a means of stripping off the mask and revealing His true divinity. If this is so, what place does the doctrine of redemption and atonement then take in the scheme of things? Has mankind really been redeemed? If so, how did Christ redeem us? It is questions like these, in various forms, which Isak Dinesen raises in her work. They are posed in the most outstanding of all her inset stories, 'The Wine of the Tetrarch', in 'The Deluge at Norderney'.[1] This story is told with a finely dramatic instinct and careful accumulation of suspense which leaves the identity of the stranger who talks with the disciple Peter concealed until the very end. When he does finally reveal that he is Barabbas, the story itself assumes all the characteristics of a parable.

After the Crucifixion Barabbas meets Peter, and tells him how his friend Phares had offered to rob a consignment of wine intended for Herod, and to give it to Barabbas in order to show the great love he bore him. Phares had indeed done this, but had been recognised later, imprisoned, and condemned to be crucified. Barabbas had managed to gain entry to the prison, and had helped Phares to escape from his cell; but when they got to the prison-wall, Barabbas was unable to climb it. Phares could have got away, if he had run, but he would not go before he had seen what was going to happen to Barabbas, and in this way they were both taken once more. Phares has now been crucified with Jesus, and Barabbas does not know what to do with his life. He had meant to revenge Phares' death, but since he is in Paradise, there is no longer any point in doing so. Therefore he has come to Peter to ask him if he may buy some of the wine Christ used

[1] This is one of the two stories told by Isak Dinesen and issued in Denmark as a gramophone record. The other is the inset story from 'Peter and Rosa'.

at the Last Supper because he has heard that this is 'very rare and has some highly precious body in it' and he feels that perhaps this will be of some help to him. Even amidst his own sorrow, Peter senses the man's affliction:

> '. . . he reflected that it might be his duty to help this man, who seemed in some deep distress. He turned to him again, but as he was looking at him it came over him that of all people in the world, this young man was the one whom he could not help. To strengthen himself he called up one of the words of the Lord himself.
> '"My son,"' he said kindly and gravely, '"take up thy cross and follow him."' The stranger, just at the same moment as the Apostle, had been about to speak. Now he stopped and looked very darkly at Peter. '"My cross! Where is my cross? Who is to take up my cross?"'[1]

Phares has laid down his life for Barabbas. And the wine for which Phares was crucified, is, for Barabbas, precisely the same as that drunk at the Last Supper symbolising Christ's blood shed for mankind. Barabbas's sense of utter futility and desolation is caused by the fact that, instead of being allowed to die with Phares, the cup had been taken from him, he had been released, and Christ had taken his cross upon Him and been crucified in his stead.

The story is told, the 'Cardinal' says, to show that 'there are worse things than perdition'; Barabbas's fate, deprived of any aim or role in life, having no cross to bear and nothing to live for, illustrates what this is. But although Barabbas figures nowhere else directly in Isak Dinesen's work, nevertheless his appearance in this story is really not an isolated occurrence. Behind all the characters, who drift through the tales unable to find a part to play, stands the archetypal figure of Barabbas. Their situation, in Isak Dinesen's art, reproduces Barabbas's own in life, deprived of a role by no less a person than Christ Himself.

When Miss Malin asks Kasparson why he had murdered the real Cardinal, he answers that 'there was little hope that both of us could be saved, and he would have sacrificed his life for mine.

[1] *Seven Gothic Tales*, p. 67.

Should I have lived on as the servant for whom the lord had died?'[1] Kasparson tells the story, 'The Wine of the Tetrarch', to underline the change his life has undergone: he has murdered the real Cardinal in order to save himself from the same fate as confronted Barabbas. He has at last found a purpose in life, and taken his redemption into his own hands—by rejecting the doctrine of atonement in refusing to allow the lord to sacrifice his own life for his servant. He faces perdition in one sense, but has found salvation in another—by becoming the self-appointed master of his own destiny. Once again a character in Isak Dinesen's tales follows the same path advocated by Yeats:

> If we cannot imagine ourselves as different from what we are, and try to assume that second self, we cannot impose a discipline upon ourselves, though we may accept one from others. Active virtue, as distinguished from the passive acceptance of a code, is therefore theatrical, consciously dramatic, the wearing of a mask.[2]

Nor is Kasparson the only character who becomes the master of his fate by rejecting the doctrine of atonement. In 'The Cardinal's Third Tale', for example, included in *Last Tales*, Father Jacopo and the proud and intransigent Lady Flora Gordon have a series of discussions about religious problems in which he tries to convert her to a Christian belief. At one point Father Jacopo draws her attention to the fact that Christ sacrificed His life for humanity by saying: '"You are aware that one is dead for us all."' Lady Flora, in turn, sharply rebuts this: '"Not for me . . . I beg to be excused! Never in my life have I asked any human being—much less any god—to die for me, and I must insist that my own personal account be kept altogether outside this statement."'[3] Kasparson also begged to be excused and to be allowed to make up his own personal account. The defiant idea behind the statement, 'never have I asked any human being—much less any god—to die for me', has a long history in Isak Dinesen's authorship and can be traced back to

---

[1] *Seven Gothic Tales*, p. 74.
[2] 'Per Amica Silentia Lunae,' *Mythologies*, p. 334.
[3] *Last Tales*, pp. 86–87.

the very early story '*Familien de Cats*'[1] (The de Cats Family)
first published in 1909, when she was twenty-four years old.

The de Cats are a family living in Amsterdam towards the end
of the eighteenth century, renowned throughout the country as a
model of righteousness and as a pattern of all the virtues. They
are only able to be this, however, because there is one individual
in each generation who acts as a scapegoat by taking upon himself all the sins which would normally be shared out amongst
the rest. This person is always banished from the family as soon
as it becomes clear that he is the one who has been singled out
for this role. At the time of the story the particular scapegoat is
Jeremias de Cats. The family agrees, however, to break its
general rule in response to the pleas of his mother, and to accept
him back into the fold. Soon after they have done this, they
begin to fall from grace. One of them takes a mistress, a young
daughter takes a lover, another marries for the sake of a distinguished name; one and all, they succumb to various tempta-
tions. Two of the brothers decide that in order to save the
entire family, Jeremias must again become the black sheep, and
try various plans to tempt him back to his former role. All are in
vain, and finally, in despair, they hold a family council. One of
the de Cats, the Bishop of Haarlem, makes a speech to the
assembly, during the course of which the role of the scapegoat
undergoes a transfiguration into that of a sublime redeemer:

'Fate, life demands a sacrifice from us today. Yes. But what does it
mean then to sacrifice and to be sacrificed? Is it a hard fate? When
it becomes necessary, it is not hard. The world's laws are just, but
they are not hard, only weakness calls them that. Let us ask, what
is it that demands a sacrifice? It is the good, virtue. Is it a hard
law to sacrifice oneself for these things? To sacrifice our lives for
virtue is the very goal towards which the best of us are striving.
Indeed, my friends, when we look at it in the right way, it is a
wonderful, a sublime fate to be sacrificed in order to save the

[1] *Tilskueren*, January, 1909. Reprinted in *Osceola*, pp. 109–140. The story
has not been translated into English, although there is an indication that at
one time Isak Dinesen thought of doing so, and including it in *Anecdotes of
Destiny*. In a note amongst her MSS, dated 29th February, 1952, there is a
table of contents for this volume, in which this tale is included under the
title of 'The de Cats' Saga'.

many. The individual bears the sins of the many upon him, their guilt is gathered together on him so that they can be justified; in order that they should live, he must be condemned. But one man's sacrifice provides the means for the salvation of the many, yea, of a whole people.'[1]

The others concur with his sentiments, but they are still unable to decide what to do. Jeremias himself arrives to rescue them from their dilemma. He offers to revert to his former ways, provided that they will agree to support him financially for the rest of his life in that station which he feels is his due. With great relief they agree to his price. Having bought their salvation, secure in their knowledge that all their sins are being borne by one man, they can now take up once more their life of virtue, with no snares spread before them, nor any temptation to deviate again from the narrow path of righteousness.[2]

The rejection of the idea of a scapegoat—or Redeemer—and the irony, directed against those who do accept this concept and live by it, is very clear in this story. And it is one which has a direct bearing upon the doctrine of redemption and atonement. If the Passion and Crucifixion were not, according to Isak Dinesen, meant to divest man of the responsibility for his own course and to take from him the necessity of working out his own destiny in life, nevertheless there is still a way left which Christ has pointed out that man should follow to find his own salvation. Another parable, similar to 'The Wine of the Tetrarch', can be found in 'The Fish', which shows what this way is.

In this parable the Lord hears of the hard conditions on earth, the lamentations of mankind at its lot, and their request that He should impart the solution to the riddle of this life. He

[1] *Osceola*, p. 133.

[2] Isak Dinesen incorporated some of the ideas from this story in 'The Dreamers' where Lincoln receives a letter from his father telling him that ' "we are, as a family, only so much better than others because we have always had amongst us one individual who has carried all the weaknesses and vice of his generation. The faults which normally would have been divided up among a whole lot of people have been gathered together upon the head of one of them only, and we others have in this way come to be what we have been, and are," ' and adds, ' "I feel I have reason to believe you the chosen victim of your generation." ' (*Seven Gothic Tales*, pp. 290–291.)

decides to assume the likeness of a man, to live in the world, and share all the conditions of mankind. After thirty-three years He returns to heaven, bearing the wounds of the Crucifixion, and tells the angels:

> 'I now know the conditions and modes of man; no one knows them better than I. I had taken pity on man, and resolved to help him, I have not rested before I had fulfilled my promise. I have now reconciled the heart of man with the conditions of the earth. I have shown this poor and unwitting creature the way to become reviled and persecuted, I have shown him how to get himself spat upon and scourged, I have taught him how to get himself hung upon a cross. I have given to man that solution of his riddle, that he begged of me, I have consigned to him his salvation.'[1]

'I have consigned to him his salvation': this is the part which Isak Dinesen sees man as playing in the scheme of things devised by God.

This can be traced in ampler detail in a criticism which she wrote of a novel, *Rytteren*,[2] (The Rider) by the Danish author, H. C. Branner. It is the only sustained piece of literary criticism Isak Dinesen wrote, and it is not surprising to find that it tells us as much about her own work as it does about Branner's. In this essay she stated her conviction that the novel was important as an epitome of the ideas and beliefs of contemporary times. The chief way in which it reflects these is through the main character, Clemens. According to her, he saves the other persons spiritually by taking their guilt from them, and redeems them by bearing it himself. Clemens consequently conforms to a pattern of behaviour which can be traced far back in time:

> The promise of redemption by blood runs through countless generations and nations. And deep in the minds of many genera-tions and nations have been rooted faith in and expectation of a miracle—the miracle of the one who alone can redeem all by taking the guilt of all upon himself . . . With great care and with the help of a very old book which he has consulted from time to time the author of *Rytteren* set himself the task of presenting the miracle of

[1] *Winter's Tales*, pp. 235–236.
[2] First published in 1949. Translated into English by A. I. Roughton and published in 1951 with the title, *The Riding Master*.

the salvation of the many by the one . . .: 'He is despised and rejected of men. Surely he hath born our griefs, and carried our sorrows, he was wounded for our transgressions, he was bruised for our iniquities.' Isaiah, 53, 5–7.[1]

This is one of the concepts in *Rytteren* which Isak Dinesen criticises so sharply:

> In the modern gospel of *Rytteren*, Clemens is the saviour, a human incarnation of the good, and he acts as a redeemer by being charitable. And in the book as long as he practises this automatic salvation with no effort on the part of those he is saving, it is more of a degradation than a redemption.[2]

She develops this point:

> The new evangelists, the Latter Day Saints, make capital out of the old evangelists, or they make capital out of Christ Himself, by introducing Him into their preaching both in disguise as well as in His own person. But there is no precedent in the Holy Scriptures of the past for this. Christ was not charitable. In His calling as a saviour He did not use the automatic salvation of the modern preachers, which has the character of a redemption carried out under an anaesthetic, does not presuppose any effort or co-operation on the part of the man to be saved, and does not require any desire or will to be saved.[3]

How radically this 'modern gospel of degradation' differs from her own, and what she means by 'active co-operation on the part of the human being' can be seen in the story 'The Heroine'.

Amongst her manuscripts there are several typescript drafts of a story called, at that stage, 'The Dreamer'. She never got much further than sketching out a rudimentary plot, but it is clear even from this that it contains the central idea from which 'The Heroine' was later developed. In the summer of 1914, a young Englishman called Henry Martineau[4] is studying

[1] *Essays*, p. 199.
[2] *Essays*, p. 203.
[3] ibid., p. 202.
[4] The name varies. In the longest draft he is called this. In another he is named Berkeley Martineau, in another, Lincoln Havergal, and in yet another, Lincoln Forssner [sic]. It seems therefore that Berkeley Cole acted as the

metallurgy in Berlin. Absorbed in his studies he is oblivious of the course which international events are taking. When he does become aware of this, he leaves for England, but only gets as far as Belgium, where he is interned after the German invasion. In his internment he finds consolation in dreams. The drafts break off with the following fragmentary sentences: 'One particular apprehension'; 'Christ died to save', 'If he could, by dying in captivity, relieve all the captives of the earth, would he do it?' The question is taken up again later in 'The Heroine', posed in much more concrete terms—and answered.

Frederick Lamond, an Englishman, is also a student in Berlin, but the time of the story has been moved back almost fifty years and it is now set in 1870 on the eve of the Franco-Prussian war. An even more significant change is that Frederick is no longer studying metallurgy, but is now studying religious philosophy, and is working upon a book on the subject of the doctrine of atonement. He, too, is immersed in his studies, hears of the imminence of war only at the last moment, leaves Berlin, but is unable to get across the German frontier and is stranded near the border with a party of French refugees, all of whom are in a state of great confusion and anxiety. The atmosphere becomes completely transformed by the arrival of the noble young French lady, Heloise. Poised and unperturbed, with an air of great hauteur and command, she 'immediately became the central figure of their small world . . . She was not in the least afraid. She met the anxiety of the pale assembly . . . with undaunted forbearance, as if she realised that they must needs have been looking forward in suspense to her arrival.'[1]

The parallel with Christ which Isak Dinesen is gradually establishing is clear (there is, however, a marked note of comedy throughout the story which prevents this parallel from appearing

[1] *Winter's Tales*, p. 73.

model for more than one of Isak Dinesen's characters. On the other hand, Frederick Lamond, the main character in 'The Heroine', has few, if any features in common with Lincoln Forsner. The most probable explanation lies in the fact that 'The Dreamer' as well as forming the germ of 'The Heroine' also represents an early stage of 'The Dreamers'.

too jarringly disproportionate). It is made even clearer when Frederick's manuscript and notes on the atonement are discovered, and the phrase from Isaiah, found amongst them, 'He was wounded for our transgressions', is interpreted as a secret code. The party are accused of being spies, and are brought before three German officers to be tried. One of them makes Heloise an offer. The whole party will be saved if she agrees to appear before him, stark-naked, to collect their passports. Heloise hesitates for a moment:

> 'Why do you ask me?' she said. 'Ask those who are with me. These are poor people, hard-working, and used to hardships. Here is a French priest . . . the consoler of many poor souls; here are two French sisters, who have nursed the sick and dying. The two others have children in France, who will fare ill without them. Their salvation is, to each one of them, more important than mine. Let them decide for me if they will buy it at your price.'[1]

They all vehemently refuse; after a time, they are released. They have a 'hurried spare meal of bread and wine' and, during this supper, Heloise 'is still the central figure of their communion, but in a new way . . . Her pride, her glory was theirs, since they had been ready to die for it.'[2] Later in the story Frederick learns the truth. He has completed his treatise on atonement, and on a visit to Paris, is taken to a music-hall by a friend: 'The climax of the whole performance was the appearance of the goddess Diana herself, with nothing on at all.'[3] It is Heloise.

If the sacrifice Jesus made was not a true one, this was also the case with Heloise. She, too, was acting a part. The request to appear naked before the German officer was one she was used to fulfilling every time she appeared in her performance, and to accede to this demand would only have entailed lapsing into her true role. But she had refused, and she explains her motives to Frederick. The party of refugees was, she says, indeed running the risk of being shot, but they were also in peril of suffering an even worse fate than they ever knew:

[1] *Winter's Tales*, p. 79.
[2] ibid., p. 81.
[3] ibid., p. 84.

'... they would have made me do as the German demanded. They would have made me do it, to save their lives, if he had put it straight to them at first, or if they had only been left to themselves. And then they would never have got over it. They would have repented it all their lives, and have held themselves to be great sinners.'[1]

Heloise put the responsibility solely upon the others, allowed them to take her at face-value, to believe that it would be a great sacrifice for her, and to decide accordingly. They could either use her as a scapegoat by demanding that she should redeem them—in which case they would live on with the conviction that they were mortal sinners; or they could refuse to do so, abide by the consequences, and then her pride and glory would become theirs also.

It is from this point that one can discern the final implications of the momentous choice, with which Isak Dinesen believes man is faced. If Barabbas is the prototype of the persons in her stories who have no part to play in life, the archetypal choice confronting man, the one from which all subsequent consequences in his life stem, hinges upon nothing less than the whole doctrine of divine redemption. This, for her, can be interpreted in two ways, and the fact that both interpretations are valid is the crucial point, since it is through this that man is given the freedom of choice and the possibility of deciding which course to adopt. In one interpretation, Christ expiated the sins of the world by atoning for them with His life. By doing this He took man's cross upon His own shoulders, and man thus becomes only a passive onlooker at the Passion and Crucifixion in which Christ played the leading part. In the other, Christ showed how each one could find his own cross, bear it himself, and take full and active responsibility for his own fate.

Amongst her manuscripts there is a long, rather discursive essay of some eighty typed pages, written in Danish during the time in Kenya, discussing the importance of ideals in life. As an epigraph to one of the chapters, entitled 'St Christopher', she appended a quotation from Jacobus de Voragine's lives of the saints, *Legenda aurea*: 'Reprobus, later St Christopher, was a

[1] *Winter's Tales*, p. 86.

Syrian chieftain of mighty strength and stature, who sought someone stronger than himself whom he could serve.' She tells the St Christopher legend, and after giving the child's words, 'Fear not, for you bear on your shoulders the One who has created the world and supports it,' she adds:

> No one can know if that really reassured Reprobus; one would be inclined to think that, when given that explanation at the very moment he was staggering in the middle of the stream, nothing could have made him more terrified. But, in any case, his quest was now over and he had found something that was mighty enough for him to be able to serve with the whole of his heart.

She then goes on to apply this to ideals in life and remarks that, like St Christopher himself, no one can object to an ideal simply on the grounds that it demands heavy sacrifice: 'St Christopher could not complain of the preternatural weight of the child he was bearing on his shoulders, for it was precisely through this fact that its divine being was revealed.'

For Isak Dinesen the heavier the cross, the more this invests life with meaning. The belief in a God whose primary attributes are loving mercy and divine forgiveness is one which, ultimately, robs life of all significance. It is this that lies behind Kasparson's cry in 'The Deluge at Norderney', 'let me, at least keep God, you tender-hearted humans', and which also underlies the old lord's criticism in 'Sorrow-Acre' of the new age of feeling which has made unto itself a God in its own image, one who is always willing to retract his fiat on the plea of mercy.

Of all Isak Dinesen's stories, it is this one that reveals most starkly the nature of life under the opposite conditions. The old lord, like the God of the Old Testament, sternly refuses to relent by softening his decree and remains obdurate to all Adam's pleas (the significance of the name, like that of the old lord needs no elaboration). Anne-Marie is not, however, atoning for her son's misdeeds—it is not even certain that he is guilty of the crime of which he has been accused—but the lord has, by his grace, allowed her to save her son's life if she fulfils the conditions he has prescribed. Isak Dinesen makes no attempt to soften their harshness, and even emphasises them in the description of Anne-Marie's ordeal and death:

> At the sound of [her son's] voice she lifted her face to him, a faint, bland shadow of surprise ran over it, but still she gave no sign of having heard what he said, so that the people round them began to wonder if the exhaustion had turned her deaf. But after a moment she slowly and waveringly raised her hand, fumbling in the air as she aimed at his face, and with her fingers touched his cheek. The cheek was wet with tears, so that at the contact her finger-tips lightly stuck to it, and she seemed unable to overcome the infinitely slight resistance or to withdraw her hand. For a minute the two looked one another in the face. Then, softly and lingeringly, like a sheaf of corn that falls to the ground, she sank forward on to the boy's shoulder, and he closed his arms round her.[1]

Isak Dinesen, it seems to me, never wrote anything finer than that. But the full meaning of 'Sorrow-Acre' and, in a way, the vindication of the lord's actions are contained in a passage where Adam sees all the events falling into place—like the process that takes place in a work of art itself—as unified parts of a pattern of significance established by life:

> He saw the ways of life, he thought, as a twined and tangled design, complicated and mazy; it was not given him or any mortal to command or control it. Life and death, happiness and woe, the past and the present, were interlaced within the pattern . . . And out of the contrasting elements concord arose. All that lived must suffer, the old man, whom he had judged hardly, had suffered, as he had watched his son die, and had dreaded the obliteration of his being,—he himself would come to know ache, tears and remorse, and, even through these, the fullness of life. So might now, to the woman in the rye-field, her ordeal be a triumphant procession . . . As now he thought of it, he knew that all his life he had sought the unity of things, the secret which connects all the phenomena of existence . . . Now they had been disclosed to him today, in the place where he had played as a child. As the song is one with the voice that sings it, as the road is one with the goal, as lovers are made one in their embrace, so is man one with his destiny, and he shall love it as himself.[2]

[1] *Winter's Tales*, pp. 68–69.
[2] ibid., pp.63–64.

If there is one passage in the whole of Isak Dinesen's work that can be singled out as summing up her beliefs, it is this. And one can see from it how her attitude to God is not one to God as a supernatural being but becomes, ultimately, an attitude to human existence and a belief in the value of life itself as offering us the possibility to manifest our own destiny. She also saw the ways of life as a twined and tangled design, and her tales reveal the extent of this. Behind them all lies Isak Dinesen's unshakeable conviction that everything that lives must suffer and that this, far from being a cause for complaint, is even a matter of grace. This was no abstract hypothesis for her—'axioms in philosophy are not axioms until they are proved upon our pulses', Keats wrote, and Isak Dinesen illustrated the force of this until the end of her life. It was surely out of her basic conviction that she was able to tell Thomas Dinesen only three days before her death that, despite all the pain, she was still able to regard the whole of her life as entirely happy. Through acceptance of the necessity of suffering, man is given the chance to reveal his indomitable qualities and to accept his fate with a defiant pride, sustained by the belief that there is an idea in life, and that his sole aim is to realise it. The person who chooses this way takes his place with Isak Dinesen herself in the communion of which she wrote in the first chapter of *Shadows on the Grass*: 'the communion of yes-sayers, . . . in love with danger, with death and with God.'

The Revenge of Truth

A MARIONETTE COMEDY

The Revenge of Truth

A MARIONETTE COMEDY

DRAMATIS PERSONAE

Abraham, a treacherous innkeeper *lansquenet*
Sabine, his daughter.
Jan Bravida, a young *lansquenet* and journalist,
    guest at the inn.
Mopsus, a potman at the inn.
Fortunio, a serving-boy.
Amiane, an errant gypsy-woman, who is
    really a kind of fairy or witch.

The action takes place in Abraham's inn

SCENE ONE

Abraham: Good Mopsus, kill Jan Bravida for me tonight. It's been a long time now since I asked you to kill anybody, my good Mopsus, so you can't say that I'm asking too much of you. It is strange, Mopsus, to think that this evening he is alive, and yet tomorrow he will be dead. This evening he isn't thinking about death at all and tomorrow his head will be full of it—and of nothing else. Oh, truly, I love death. It's the only thing we have left from the greatness of past times; without death no one could stand the boredom of life. What a democrat you are, Death, my comrade, you practise true equality. Oh, let all democrats go and lie down when death comes. 'What,' says Death, 'do you complain that king Rameses and Henry Ford have been richer than you for fifty years, when I shall grant you equal incomes for the next five million years?' 'Do you talk about future states, children?' he says. 'Don't quarrel, don't quarrel about that. My future state is all the future you have, and I will carry you thither.' 'I will teach you fraternity, brothers,' Death says, 'the head of one man shall be no higher than that of any other, and there shall be no ill will between you.' 'And now abideth,' says Death, 'liberty, equality and fraternity, these three, but the greatest of these will be fraternity.' Death, the Paragon of Democracy, has yet another gift, and that is silence. What a relief it will be, when we are all silent. Wait until he's asleep, Mopsus, wait until he's asleep. Yes, be sensible. I, too, have got some business to do with Meindert Hobtoma, good business. Oh, but if only you were a little more intelligent.

Mopsus: I don't complain, master, about my not being more intelligent, but I am sorry that I am not braver. Unfortunately, I am so nervous, master, from what you have just said that I have been made quite upset. As a matter of fact, for someone like me it is wrong to be a thief and a murderer. What takes place in the dark—in that line anyway—isn't really my strong point. I shudder, master, at the thought, and if one night at long last you have nothing to do, then your conscience is a night-animal —like a badger, for instance, in the daytime it keeps quiet, but it gets bolder at night. Oh, it is really very unpleasant. I don't love death, master, I love life. I would much rather give a human being life than death, and I wish that was the task you want me to do so much, master. If only I could be certain that other people had as much of a conscience as I have. But look here, a young mercenary, and a journalist into the bargain, do you think that he would hesitate to kill a little potman? That is what worries me. Master, master, when will you begin to repent of all my sins, for *you* are the one who has always profited from them?

Abraham: Be quiet, Mopsus, someone is coming.

SCENE TWO

Amiane : Good evening, my dear children. The moon is rising, how are you?

Abraham : I don't know who you are. Have you come to have supper at the inn, or have you come to beg?

Amiane : I have come to tell you the truth.

Abraham : The truth? I'm not afraid of your threats. Sit down then and tell it.

Amiane (sitting down). You are one of the ideas of Nature and they are all wise. The woods where I come from are Nature's ideas as well, they are her deep thoughts, and the cows in the pastures are good and pretty fancies. Even every individual member of the audience in the theatre may be thought of as one of the ideas of Nature, although, considered as an audience, they aren't really, for there are limits to everything.

Abraham : Old woman, what egotism to demand that others should listen just because you want to speak.

Amiane : Some people do things they don't want to do, and they forget what they themselves really are. They upset the ideas of Nature, they make her clear wells muddy, beware of them! In the dark, throughout the night, the trees in the woods are growing. If there is a wind blowing, the tops of the trees sway in it. Such people, as I am talking about, wake at night, become anxious, and feel ashamed when they think about it.

Abraham : I can see that you are a soothsayer like all the rest. From them one has everything to fear but the truth.

Amiane : The truth is that we are all acting in a marionette comedy.

Abraham : Oh, what old clichés!

Amiane : My children, what is more important than anything else in a marionette comedy is to keep the author's idea clear. I will tell you, even though it is a secret, that this is the real happiness which people seek everywhere else. To act in a marionette comedy is a true blessing, and now that at long last I have come into one, I will never go out of it again. But you, my fellow actors, keep the author's idea clear. Aye, drive it to its utmost consequence.

Abraham: Wouldn't it be doing a good deed to report you to the archdeacon? Everybody is clamouring for more censorship.

Amiane: Good deeds are like little children. If you think too much about them they never come to anything, but when you are only full of the joys of life, and have no real intentions, you manage to create them without thinking about it.

Mopsus: You talk as though you were from the nineteenth century.

Amiane: With you I have the best of intentions and I will teach you something new. In our day everybody longs for witchcraft and they need it to be happy. Now, I am going to weave a spell, so listen carefully, for the whole point of the comedy lies in this. It is dark in the woods and in the meadows, the owls are hooting —can you hear them? I shall keep to darkness and to truth, for I guard the roots, and every living thing needs those two qualities for its own roots. You, you rich old miser, who do not recognise the truth when you see it, every lie told in your inn tonight shall be turned into truth before sunrise tomorrow morning. Only then will the spell be broken. Now children, farewell! May your affairs prosper! (She whistles. A goat enters and she gets up on its back.)

> The tree-tops in the woods are rocking gently,
> The waters of the spring are flowing softly.
> Quietly, quietly, the wood opens its heart,
> The sound and bustle of the day vanishes.

And now I must go. Perhaps I shall return, but not in this play. (She rides away.)

SCENE THREE

Abraham: Oh Lord, Thou who canst create mountains and rubber plantations whenever Thou wilt, Thou who created the prophets, why didst Thou create that old woman? What did she say, Mopsus?

Mopsus: You rich miser. You rich old miser.

Abraham: How can you possibly believe that I am rich? Tell me the truth now, Mopsus, have *you* spread that rumour?

Mopsus: Master, be careful! Remember the old woman's spell. If it isn't true, it will become so—so then, what should I say?

Abraham: I'm not rich, Mopsus. Do you see those chests over there, they're empty.

Mopsus: Yes, Master, I can see them.

Abraham: Oh what a life, what misery!

Mopsus: Have you really got anything more to say to me, master?

Abraham: No.

Mopsus: I must go.

Abraham: Go, go! Sabine!

Sabine: What do you want?

Abraham: Come in here, Sabine. We must have a young woman on the stage now, or the audience will lose patience.

SCENE FOUR

Sabine: I just don't care at all. I despise audiences. Jan Bravida has told me about them, they only come here to be mentioned in the reviews of the first night performance. I tell you, father, I'm unhappy here, and I won't go on being unhappy. I'm disgusted with life in Edam in the same way as I am with a dress that doesn't fit me. I'll find peace only when you're all dead. Last winter I even wished I was dead myself, and I took pleasure in imagining how terribly you would miss me. But that's over now. The rest of you can die, and then, free of you at last, I'll walk alone on the grass and by the sea and watch the dolphins leaping in the water. Yes, I am a girl who could have her own carriage in Paris and a box at the opera. I can't bear to live among the people in Edam, they look at me for a long, long time, then they just close their eyes and go home to their wives.

Abraham: How much cleverer they are than you, Sabine. Life is like that.

Sabine: I don't care. But why did you call me?

Abraham: Would you like a pair of pretty earrings? Jan Bravida means to leave this evening, but if you can persuade him to stay here overnight, you shall have a pair of pretty earrings tomorrow.

Sabine: For his money?

Abraham: Yes.

Sabine: I wish you luck. But you mustn't bury him under the window, I have just sown poppies there.

Abraham: My good child! We'll go into the field. (Exit.)

SCENE FIVE

Sabine (walks over to the mirror): If I am to have a pair of earrings, I prefer emerald ones. I remember that once the Countess of Brabant had a pair of emerald earrings. There's nothing that suits my complexion better than green, and it's not everybody can say that. To match them I must have a black dress, cut low, and a green bandeau round my head. When father kills Jan Bravida, he will have enough money to buy me a corset as well, even though they say that they're making frocks in Paris now without any corset at all. Would to God it were true, for anyone can buy a corset, the important thing is what goes into it.

SCENE SIX

(Fortunio walks across the room carrying a pile of plates)

Sabine (sees him in the mirror): Is that you, Fortunio?

Fortunio: Yes.

Sabine: Come and help me, I must string my pearls.

Fortunio: That really will be a pleasure. (They sit down facing each other and begin to string the pearls.)

Sabine: Tell me, Fortunio, can you ever be bothered to read any books?

Fortunio: Yes, the very latest ones. Especially the Symbolists.

Sabine: I have been wondering if you don't really get to know life best by reading those authors who have really lived life.

Don't you think you can get experience without having to suffer for it? You could sit very quietly, for instance, on the bed of a lake, if you were rich and could have a house built entirely of glass on the bottom. There you could read about crimes and passions, all the most terrible things, and yet be completely unmoved by them.

Fortunio: One could have lived ten times, have experienced other people's lives, and yet remain quite young.

Sabine: Yes, Fortunio, and have been in love many times, had children, killed them, and be just as slim as ever.

Fortunio: If a book had been written, in which we loved one another, I could have been yours, kissed you, Sabine, and yet sit here with you today stringing pearls.

Sabine: Can't you sing me a song, Fortunio?

Fortunio: Yes, whatever you like. (He sings.)

> Come sweet sorrow, come suffering, come!
> I care little for happiness,
> I found it easily, forsook it easily.
> I am tired of laughter and of smiles.
> Because of the troubles of the day,
> Who would not seek the embrace of night?
> Be still, my heart, be still,
> Tears and sorrows await you.
>
> The day before yesterday I lay in your lap,
> Yesterday I was your red rose.
> When I am dead, and laid in the earth,
> Another will buy you with gold.
> Hark! Hark! The bell is tolling.
> All paths lead but to the grave.
> Pleasures and flattery, oh, haste away,
> Come, sweet faithful sorrow, oh, return.

Sabine: You have a sweet voice, Fortunio, and that is a beautiful song. I'll give you some money tomorrow, so that you can take singing-lessons. Remind me about it. Look, now we've finished and I'll put the pearls on. Someone's coming outside, who is it?

Fortunio (looking out): It's Jan Bravida.

Sabine: Is it really Jan Bravida? Then I had better go in and take off my fichu. Goodbye, Fortunio. (Exit.)

SCENE SEVEN

Fortunio: It's Mopsus coming first, I'll wait for him. Just imagine, she's taking her fichu off for Jan Bravida. Now God help me, for there is not one girl in the whole world who would take anything off for my sake. Oh no, the times, even the century itself, must change before it is worth living. We have our cars so we can drive somewhere quickly and have tea, just as if we were in pursuit of our worst enemy, but we certainly can't slay our worst enemies. We don't even have enemies. When we hate a man, we can get him sentenced to three months' imprisonment, and when we love a woman, we can marry her. Oh, that this might be changed! (He drinks.) May it soon be changed!

SCENE EIGHT

Mopsus: You here, what are you doing here, shouldn't you be doing the washing-up?
Fortunio: I'm waiting for you, we have to act in a scene together.
Mopsus: Which scene is that?
Fortunio: The one in which I tell you that Abraham has asked me to dig a grave in the field under the pear-tree in blossom. I ask you to help me, and we talk about life after death. It's necessary for the harmony of the plot.
Mopsus: Yes, that's right, I remember that scene. It's a terribly boring one, let's skip it. (Exeunt).

SCENE NINE

Sabine: Good evening.
Jan Bravida: Good evening, oh, is it you?

Sabine: They tell me you're going away, is that true?

Jan Bravida: Couldn't you give me a glass of wine, Sabine? My head feels so awful. Lord, how tired I am! It's your father's wine. The Lord alone knows what he puts into it.

Sabine: Why do you drink so much? You lose your good looks everytime you get drunk, it harms your complexion. Here's some really old port, it's the best thing for the wine you've drunk.

Jan Bravida: I don't drink any more than I need to. I am a human being, Sabine, not even my heart can live on air alone.

Sabine: But won't you tell me why you are going away?

Jan Bravida: Because there's a girl in Antwerp who's expecting me, and who has been booked for tonight.

Sabine: In Antwerp? Do you love her?

Jan Bravida: Yes.

Sabine: More than you love me?

Jan Bravida: No. There's no one I love more than you.

Sabine: Then you shouldn't go away.

Jan Bravida: Well, why not? *You* can't make love. You girls have read so much that we men haven't. There's nothing in the world that you haven't experienced—in your imagination—and then you're afraid that it won't be so wonderful when you try it out in reality. But don't you know that theory is the only evil, practice the real good, and that a piece of dry bread, Sabine, does more to satisfy your hunger than a whole cookery-book?

Sabine: No, I don't know that, will you teach me, Jan Bravida?

Jan Bravida: Yes, come on, I'll share my last piece with you.

Sabine: And yet, do you really know something? I wonder if you will think of me this time tomorrow.

Jan Bravida: Yes. You are so beautiful and so sweet, Sabine, I believe I could love you for always.

Sabine: Yes, just as long as you live. But, dear Jan Bravida, your words of love have a warmed-up taste, do your kisses taste the same? Go to Antwerp, there you will find that when they talk about kissing, they mean exactly that kind.

Jan Bravida: You mustn't be so affected, Sabine, and don't talk

about things you don't understand. I think you would be satisfied with me—everyone has been. When you are mine, I'll be
faithful to you, and not even look at other girls. I'm already tired
of wine and gambling.

Sabine: If I kissed you now, Jan Bravida, would you be satisfied
with that kiss and then go away? If so, then kiss me and go, and
let us hope she will be sweet and kind to you.

Jan Bravida: No, I won't go, I'll stay here.

Sabine: Without making any conditions?

Jan Bravida: Yes.

Sabine: Oh Jan Bravida, is that girl in Antwerp pretty? How
you must love me! God will reward you, and so shall I.

Jan Bravida: Will you give me some more wine?

Sabine: Yes.

Jan Bravida: I've got to review a première for tomorrow's
paper. If you help me, Sabine, I'll finish it more quickly.

Sabine: What kind of première is it?

Jan Bravida: This one, Sabine. Look out there, and tell me who
are sitting in the stalls.

Sabine: Oh, Jan Bravida, don't talk like that. You know very
well who are in the stalls.

Jan Bravida: Yes, I know, and they all know. But what can we
do about it? You're full of affectations, Sabine, but I'm a modern
young man and have a matter-of-fact attitude to life. I have to
write from the stalls about the people who are in the stalls, and
since they are always the same, I must always write about the
same people. But can that harm anyone?

Sabine: But why do you write about that?

Jan Bravida: What did you say?

Sabine: But why do you write about that?

Jan Bravida: You're lucky to be able to ask that. I've got to do
it, Sabine, I have to, for the sake of the public, only they mustn't
find out about it. They pay me a high salary never to find out.
Do you think that it amuses me to go to the races at Klampenborg, Sabine? It's often quite awful, you know, but I go to
them, and that is why the public loves me. Yes, they love me
because, since I got that newspaper-column, they can believe
that the races are enjoyable, that the first nights at the theatre

are enjoyable, that even the winter-carnivals are enjoyable. Without me they simply could not bear the pleasures of their existence. I don't specialise in pity, Sabine, there's another columnist who does that. And yet I do feel pity for the public. They can't help it that they no longer believe in life everlasting, and yet they need something to look forward to, something which goes beyond the present. So they look to me, for they know that I'll write about them in tomorrow's review.

Sabine: You really shouldn't complain. When the prettiest girls put on their hats and go to the races, they think of you—and of their lovers.

Jan Bravida: Yes, because they know that I am kind-hearted. I'm glad that I am, Sabine. People here in Edam, Sabine, love corruption, you know, the corruption of the times—and they also love a kind heart. They cannot do without either of those two things, and that's how you can recognise them. They're no longer afraid of me; whatever I do, they say to one another, 'he's so impertinent, but he's kind-hearted'. Tell me now who is in the stalls?

Sabine: Oh my angel, put off writing that review, I think it must be an awful job to be a journalist.

Jan Bravida: What shall we do then, Sabine?

Sabine: Let's talk about making love.

Jan Bravida: Oh my darling, there's nothing to *talk* about.

Sabine: Don't you believe that I can love, dearest? There's no girl in the Netherlands who can love like me.

Jan Bravida: Do you think so? Have you been to Antwerp?

Sabine: Speak properly to me, Jan Bravida, and don't tease me. There are a lot of girls who make eyes at people, but to make love to them must really be something terribly insipid. We're only young once, and youth is soon gone. Somehow everything is beautiful, look how bright the moon is. And you can see it in the canal. I don't know why, but I think there's still something missing from my happiness.

Jan Bravida: Yes, that you love me, that's the only thing.

Sabine: It would be wonderful if I loved you, and you loved me, it would be just like it is in old plays. What would happen then, Jan Bravida?

Jan Bravida: Then I would come over to you, Sabine, (going to her), and kneel in front of you (kneeling), and put my head on your knee, (doing so), and say to you, 'You should try to love me. Your life is nothing but foolery, you don't know what it is to love. But my darling, it's so wonderful, to love you is like walking in a meadow full of flowers, no, in a wood where all the birds are singing.'

Sabine: Oh my sweet, sweet, Jan Bravida. You would be intoxicated by your own words, if you weren't drunk already.

Jan Bravida: Oh, you mustn't mind that. Don't you know that when you keep talking about something, you end up by thinking of it? We've written so many articles about the poor little children that, in the end, the new law about alimony will be passed and so we must think about them. But the moon is so bright this evening that you think about everything which is white and beautiful. Won't you love me, Sabine?

Sabine: Do you really love me, my dear?

Jan Bravida: Yes, I, who know what love is like, you can see that I can't let you go. I won't do you any harm, but I love you. There is no ecstasy, no battle, no race, that can be compared to love, not even dancing or moonlight, Sabine, which your sort of people like so much. If I could explain it to you properly, you would love me.

Sabine: You sound almost like my mother did, when she was alive.

Jan Bravida: Dear, sweet Sabine, let your hands stay there.

Sabine: No; but she said, 'only love is truth, everything else is delusion'. Would you like me to love you?

Jan Bravida: Yes, I would.

Sabine: I love you. Since the first time I saw you
The fairies have been playing wherever I went.
Because dreams are to fairies
What flowers are to butterflies.

I read that in a book, you know.

Jan Bravida: I've never loved anyone else but you. Even if anyone says so, don't believe it. You are wonderful, Sabine, I care for nothing in the world but you.

Sabine: I love you. My heart understands
Your heart without need for words,
Like the grass does the summer rain.

Jan Bravida: Oh you are so beautiful, Sabine. If you really meant what you just said, I would die for you.

Sabine: Would you die for me? You're also handsome, in a way. God grant, Jan Bravida, that this moment last for ever. Let me tidy your hair, it's so ruffled. What are you thinking about now under all that hair?

Jan Bravida: That I want to kiss you.

Sabine: No, I don't want to kiss you. I was told once that if you love and kiss someone, he knows all your secret thoughts immediately. I could easily kiss you without loving you, and I could easily love you without kissing you, but I am very modern in my ideas, and I wonder if I could both kiss you *and* love you? And if I kissed you once, I might just as well go on, but if I kiss you all night, you will certainly die tomorrow morning, sweet Jan Bravida.

Jan Bravida: No, when I get to know all your secrets, you won't let me die tomorrow morning. You'll find out that it's a good thing, if there's one person in the world who knows them.

Sabine: No, perhaps I won't, it's not easy to say. You don't know how much I treasure you. Look at me, let my heart drink from your wonderful eyes, let me come deep into your heart and feel your thoughts wrapping around me. If I loved you, I would say, 'Now let misfortune come when it will, I still have you.'

Jan Bravida: Let me wake in your young and peaceful arms in the morning and think that I will love you for ever.

Sabine: How much must you give that girl in Antwerp?

Jan Bravida: One hundred guilders.

Sabine: Oh, I'm still of some use to you . . . You're saving a hundred guilders by staying with me tonight.

Jan Bravida: It's so hot here, come, let me carry you outside.

Sabine: Yes, under the pear-tree in blossom in the meadow.

Jan Bravida: Yes. Do you love me?

Sabine: Yes, and do you love me?

Jan Bravida: You don't need to ask. Yes, I love you, Sabine, I adore you.

Sabine: Then don't let go of me. I've been born only for this one night. Oh, I've only this, only you, my Jan Bravida, all, all the years have been made for this. Because I love you, I understand everything now, all creatures, the grass, dreams, the whole world. I will love you all my life because you have taught me how sweet and wonderful it is to be alive and to be in love, but especially because I love you, yes, I love you. Oh my dear, how strong you are. How can you be in love with me? Oh my dear.

Jan Bravida: Sabine, kiss me.

Sabine: There's the nightingale now. Hark!

Jan Bravida: Oh Sabine, kiss me.

Sabine: Yes, but tell me first, do you think green earrings will suit me?

Jan Bravida: Yes, they will.

Sabine: Oh come, kiss me.

Jan Bravida (kissing her)*:* I love you.

Sabine: I love you.

Jan Bravida (kissing her)*:* For ever, Sabine?

Sabine: Always. God! Oh good God! (Exit.)

SCENE TEN

Jan Bravida: Has she gone? Will she come back? If she doesn't come, I won't live any longer. God! Let her come back again tonight and I'll always be faithful to her, I will do everything she wants me to. Oh I can't bear this terrible doubt and uncertainty for long. Let me see. At midnight the whole of Abraham's house should be still; what's the time now? (A clock strikes) Half-past eleven. For three-quarters of an hour I'll believe she'll come, or else I'll live no longer. Under the pear-tree in the meadow, under that pear-tree in blossom, and then I won't drink any more and never kiss another girl. It's nothing but foolery to do so, and life should be something more than just that, shouldn't it? Oh, with you Sabine, I'll really live. Everything will be different. Oh, her shoulders, her eyes, her limbs!

SCENE ELEVEN

Jan Bravida: Come Mopsus, let us play *labraveuse.*
Mopsus: Yes. I came in here, sir, because I wondered if you'd like to have my company, and so I thought I'd sit here and we could talk about deep and serious subjects. The people I mix with have a great influence on me, so I really do need good company, but I don't often get it.
Jan Bravida: Don't you often get it here? Draw.
Mopsus: Yes, red. So you get the black, sir, that was a strange coincidence. Drink, good sir, it gives one courage, and yet *you* don't need it, but I do. Will you let me drink a glass of that wine? I always drink it when I get the chance. It's as good as a complete sermon on the text that you should, above all, look after your stomach, since a good mood comes from the stomach.
Jan Bravida (his reply is thought to mar the scene so it is omitted).
Mopsus: You're in high spirits, good sir. You probably have good reason to be?
Jan Bravida (thoughtfully)*:* Yes, because the moon is shining so brightly.
Mopsus: Yes, it's quite beautiful, and yet it's rather strange that it can make a person cheerful, since it isn't really an advantage. But I have often thought that therefore God loves us like we love our dogs, for when he is in high spirits, we are in high spirits, and when he is in a bad mood, we are also sad at heart. On this bright, moonlight night God is in an elegiac mood, and we trot at his heels as best we can. God knows, sir, I'm very disturbed this evening, especially about you, but you mustn't feel offended about it.
Jan Bravida: No, God knows, Mopsus, you may have your reasons.
Mopsus: I'll tell you my story. You probably come from martial stock?
Jan Bravida: Yes.
Mopsus: But not everybody is hatched out of an eagle's egg and wants only battle and soaring flight, there are also some who are

born sheep, you know, the sheep themselves. My mother was chief laundress to the Archdeacon in Oppendam, my father was the skating-club, 'Altid frejdig'[1], in Haarlem. My mother was one of the old school, only on her deathbed did she tell me the club's name.

Jan Bravida: No, is that true, Mopsus? My uncle, the Bishop of Haarlem, when he was young, was president of that club, and it was he who chose its name.

Mopsus: Really, that's strange, sir. Yes, it's a small world. But, to go on, my mother was very strict. She pestered me with her morality, and it has always been a comfort to me, that when anything in life went wrong, it has shown that my upbringing was a complete misunderstanding.

Jan Bravida: And so was mine.

Mopsus: When I grew up, my conscience was my greatest trial. Even at this moment, sir, I shudder when I think of it. Tell me, when you have killed someone, have you repented much of it?

Jan Bravida: No Mopsus, it's not me who created the world. Only God can know what he was thinking of when he did so. Mopsus, look at the clock, is it soon midnight?

Mopsus: Sir, why do you want to know that? No, sir, there's another twenty minutes.

Jan Bravida: Give me some more wine, Mopsus.

Mopsus: Yes sir, let us drink some more wine. Your health, good sir. Ah, alas, you have your love-affairs, and a large debt, and perhaps you're ill, and you think that I have no sorrows because I'm so fat. But I'll tell you something so you can pity me, sir, oh, I'm so glad when someone pities me.

Jan Bravida: I'm winning, Mopsus. I've won fifteen guilders.

Mopsus: God bless you, sir, may you go on winning for as long as you want to. Sir, I'm the one that has written the play.

Jan Bravida: What play?

Mopsus: This play, Jan Bravida, and I don't mind telling you that I'm very satisfied indeed with it. I think I've been successful in everything except for my own character. Isn't it awful to have been successful in everything and to have presented everything clearly, except for one's own character? I can tell you, my

---

[1] 'Nothing daunted', the title of a hymn in Danish.

hair stands on end when I remember that we have only seven scenes left. But, you know, Jan Bravida, I'm going to sacrifice the whole plot in order to make my own character clear in those seven scenes. Ah, what did I say? The terrible fate of the artist is that I can't do that. I love you all better than I do myself, I, the one who ought to love myself. Oh, let it be entered into your account, as at some time it will into mine—he loved these puppets better than himself, for their characters he sacrificed his own soul.

Jan Bravida: What time is it, Mopsus?

Mopsus: Ten to twelve, sir.

Jan Bravida: The game is finished, Mopsus, and I've won, but I can't follow your profound remarks any longer. Goodnight, Mopsus. (Exit.)

SCENE TWELVE

Mopsus (during this scene he produces a skeleton-key, opens Abraham's chests, and empties the money into a sack): The worst risk I can now run is if there should be a just Providence. But even at the worst, even at this moment, it is very likely he would consider me from the point of view that it is better to be unfaithful to my master and take this useless money from him, than to be faithful to him and kill Jan Bravida. The difficulty about doing God's will is that I can never be certain about his character. I do what Abraham wants me to do, as far as possible, because I like to get on with him. But God knows there is no one I would better like to get on with than with God himself. Yes, it is God who is fundamentally my sole interest, and that is the only reason why I am so interested in mankind. They are his creation, and could help me understand his character, but then there are so many different sides to him. If I were certain that he had absolutely no sense of humour, I would gladly sacrifice the little wit I have. But I just can't believe that. No. But is it possible that God is nothing but a humorist? Dear Lord, if Thou hast any humour, then look upon me with humour. But if Thou art in deadly earnest and Thy seriousness has no limits, oh, Thou eternal, Thou sublime One, let us, Thou and I, take that little potman, Mopsus, in Edam, whom all the rest either laugh or smile at, with quite, quite deadly seriousness. Amen.

SCENE THIRTEEN

Sabine: Mopsus, thou shalt not steal.
Mopsus: Oh good God, almighty God!
Sabine: How bad you are, that is very wicked.
Mopsus: Why do you say that? For merciful God's sake, explain why you come here and say that.
Sabine: You must call him now.
Mopsus: No! Who?
Sabine: Jan Bravida. 'Who?' says Mopsus! Call Jan Bravida.
Mopsus: Ah Sabine, now I understand you. How old are you? Twenty. Yes really, isn't that just wonderful.
Sabine: Absolutely, Mopsus. Lord, how I love him. Of course nothing whatever bad must happen to him.
Mopsus: No—so you think so, too? And I'm not stealing from him.
Sabine: No, I can see that they're my father's chests. Dear Mopsus, call him.
Mopsus: Shall I? Shan't I? I'm quite bewildered and I can't cope with two plans at the same time.
Sabine: Mopsus, have you killed him?
Mopsus: No, of course not. God save me! Dear Sabine.
Sabine: Jan Bravida! Jan Bravida!
Mopsus: I wonder whether this is lucky or unlucky for me? I'll stay quite still.

SCENE FOURTEEN

Jan Bravida: Oh Sabine, my angel, my angel, how sweet, how sweet of you to come.

Sabine: Oh Jan Bravida, kiss me.

Jan Bravida: I didn't think you would come, Sabine. I would have died if you hadn't. My darling, oh, my darling!

Sabine: But you must go away. Listen, my father wants to kill you for your money and bury you in the field. Your grave has already been dug, and I was to get a pair of earrings for your money.

Jan Bravida: Were you? But you're so beautiful, Sabine.

Sabine: Now listen. My father told me to see that you stayed here tonight. That was the reason why I kissed you. I knew that you were going to die, and when I kissed you, I thought, there are only five hours left until the morning.

Jan Bravida: Then why do you come and tell me now, Sabine? Oh tell me, why have you come?

Sabine: Do you ask that? Well then, listen. Because I love you. You knew that, didn't you? Now you do then. Oh Jan Bravida, don't think it's you I'm laughing at. God must hear I'm laughing. Was five hours enough? But you must hurry and leave here.

Jan Bravida: Yes, and I'll take you with me. Will you go with me always, Sabine?

Sabine: Wherever in the world you go. My hands shall be yours, my hopes shall be yours, take everything, my dear one, I'll give you everything.

Jan Bravida: Oh lift me up, hold me close, kiss me like rain falling on a summer's night.

Sabine: Your hair is like a wild horse's mane, you shall have no cares in the world.

Jan Bravida: Your hair smells like flowers on the moor.

Sabine: Strong Jan Bravida, you shall have no wishes in the whole world left unfulfilled.

Jan Bravida: Oh Sabina, you are so warm and your skin is so smooth. There is salvation for everything with you.

Mopsus: Do you mind my asking if you're really thinking of leaving?

Sabine: Yes we are, Mopsus.

Mopsus: Well then, I'll go too. I don't want to be here when Abraham finds out that I haven't killed Jan Bravida, but instead he has run off with his daughter, and that certain other things have happened as well.

Sabine : Come, let us saddle 'Garrow Hill'. I can ride on the mule and I must take some packages with me.

Mopsus : Are you going? Don't go. I think, in fact, I'm quite certain that the clock will strike twelve now, and Abraham will come. All right, I won't say a word when he questions me.

Jan Bravida : Can you ride, Sabine? That mule will throw you off. We can take the road to Antwerp, to the next inn, 'Naboth's Vineyard'.

Sabine : No, not to 'Naboth's Vineyard', that's our worst rival. All right, it doesn't matter now. (The clock strikes twelve.)

Mopsus : Listen. Oh, I don't understand why *I* always get such terrible pangs of conscience when other people never do. God grant that the clock would soon finish striking.

Sabine : Someone's coming.

Mopsus : Yes.

Sabine : Put the light out, and let's go. (Exeunt Jan Bravida and Sabine.)

SCENE FIFTEEN

Abraham : Mopsus, are you here?

Mopsus : Yes.

Abraham : Have you done your duty, Mopsus?

Mopsus : Yes.

Abraham : Was it easy?

Mopsus : Yes.

Abraham : All right then, come here. Fortunio is with me, let's carry him out and bury him.

Mopsus : No master, we can't bury him, because I haven't killed him.

Abraham : Why not?

Mopsus : We're all weak, master. I would have done it, master, but my will wasn't strong enough. Even this morning when I was talking to you, I doubted if it would be strong enough, but I still hoped, but the hope was mistaken, master.

Abraham: Fortunio, bring the lantern.

Mopsus: Let me tell you the whole truth, master. He's in love with your daughter, and far from meaning to help us kill him, she has helped him get away. They've taken the mule with them. Your chests here, master, have been broken into, and what there was in them—whether there was anything or not—has been taken away.

Abraham: Oh my heart, my poor heart! Fortunio, come here and help me. (*Fortunio brings the lantern.*)

Mopsus: Oh dear master, your daughter and your son-in-law will get no happiness from this money.

Abraham: My daughter. My money.

Mopsus: Ah master, never put your trust in treasures, which moth and rust doth corrupt, nor in young daughters who thieves break through and steal.

Abraham: Do you know, Mopsus, I think you are lying. They have not taken the money.

Mopsus: Why not?

Abraham: Haven't *you* got it?

Mopsus: No, I haven't. God alone knows where it is. Master, I am honest, I believe what people tell me. Look, when you told me this morning that your chests were empty, I believed you.

Abraham: What have you got in that sack, Mopsus, that you're holding behind your back?

Mopsus: I can't open it, master.

Abraham: Ha, Mopsus, I thought you were my faithful and clever dog; how badly you lie. Give me that sack, open it.

Mopsus: Let me speak a moment, master. Do you remember there are bats hanging in our cellar, our deep cellar, where you never allow a living stranger to go down? You don't like them, master, and the last time we were down there, you were carrying the head and went first, and you ran your head into them, for they were hanging down from the ceiling as if they were dead, and their dry, cold and sticky bodies brushed against your forehead. You shrieked out aloud, master. I really am your faithful and clever dog, master, I summoned up all my courage and affection for you, and went down there, gathered them up, and put them into a sack to burn them. That was in the day-time, master, while they were asleep, but at night—and now it is midnight—they wake up, you could say, like ghosts. If I open the sack now, they will swarm out, and who knows what they have been eating, one of them could get into your beard. Shall I open it, master?

Abraham: Yes, Mopsus, open it. Oh, Mopsus, Mopsus, only Fortunio, you and I know that cellar, only he, you and I will go down there again, and *then* you will find out what your bats eat.

Mopsus: If I now give in to you, master, all my trouble has been wasted. Think of that another time when you start to judge me. (He opens the sack and a large number of bats fly out of it, scatter over the stage, and fly away.)

Mopsus: Do you see, master?

Abraham: Oh mad world! My money gone, my chests empty, why should I waste more words on this audience, which doesn't understand me, and on this comedy, where everything has turned out badly for me, even though it could just as easily have turned out well. In fact everything would have been more original like that. Away, away. Fortunio, give me that lantern. Perhaps I still have a chance of catching the thieves.

Mopsus: It's no use, master, it's no use. You'll never see your money again.

SCENE SIXTEEN

Mopsus: God, I have done you an injustice, I knew of course you could perform miracles if you wanted to, but I didn't believe you had a feeling for that kind. There was something very charming in letting that little prophecy come true. I see how generous you are, I believe everything is possible, why, I could even believe in the forgiveness of sins.

Fortunio: Hadn't you stolen Abraham's money then?

Mopsus: No, I haven't stolen it, Fortunio. Neither have I killed the old pedlar with the woolpack, who was here last year, nor have I seduced the landlord's daughter and she never had twins. I didn't steal rock-candy when I was a grocer's apprentice, and as a youth, I didn't let myself be persuaded to do anything at all by the Lord High Steward to the Court. Isn't that nice? Oh, my soul is so light it is flying skywards like a lark. How white and clean I am, like newly ironed linen.

SCENE SEVENTEEN

Sabine: I saw my father running across the fields carrying a lantern. What did he say, Mopsus?

Mopsus: It would be so difficult to explain, Sabine, and you wouldn't really care to hear about it.

Jan Bravida: Is this scene a long one? Let's get away.

Mopsus: Yes, and since I'm independent now, I'll go with you. I can't tell you how glad I am to be finished with stealing and murdering now, and especially to be free from the voice of conscience.

Fortunio: Oh, and what about me?

Sabine: What Fortunio, are you crying? Oh, don't cry.

Fortunio: I'm crying because you're going away, and soon everything will be over. Oh, is the whole play over? Do you remember the little scene the two of us were in together? I strung your pearls and sang for you while the moon was rising. And now in a moment the curtain will fall and everything will be over, and there is no mortal power which can call us back here. My role in this was a fine one, I liked it, and when it is over tonight, who knows what role I'll get?

Sabine: Well, Fortunio, don't be sad, we have done our best, and we don't ask to do more than that. When we first began, no one knew what his role was like, indeed, we ourselves didn't know, for who can know what a character will look like on the stage? But now we have said those lines we had in us, we haven't kept a single one back, and when the curtain falls, no one can have any doubt what we really were. Oh I hope that sometime each member of the audience will be able to say the same thing!

Fortunio: Will you take me with you?

Sabina: Yes, a little way, Fortunio. We'll all of us go together out of this comedy. And he will find some comfort in Antwerp,

won't he? We'll all be happy. But Fortunio, haven't you got a
song left, and won't you sing it before we leave.
Fortunio : Yes, but is it worth singing? It's that kind of song,
which sounds very nice, but really hasn't any meaning.
(Singing):

> Weigh anchor and let us sail,
> Steer toward the open sea.
>
> The breeze carries a sweet scent with it,
> Island after island becomes a lovely green.
>
> But oh, the salt, rolling sea,
> Stretching boundless.
> And oh, the wild breezes winding
> Their paths in the air and singing
> All earthly woes are brief.
>
> The seas and the wide heavens embrace us,
> Our boat is sailing into Eternity.
> We are young to sail,
> To love,
> To let the heart skim
> Like a boat before the wind and the showers,
> To feel the cheek wet with the tears and the
> kisses of the sea.

> Oh, beautiful maidens are going
> With ribbons in their long hair
> Over meadows and over moors,
> Gathering corn and picking roses.
>
> But the groves have no sweet kisses
> Like the open seas at dawn.
> And no embrace in the world is so blissful
> As the one when the sea is rolling far under the
> ship and your berth.
> Even cradling my shoulder on yours
> Deep as our hearts.

Hoist the sail. Oh Hope, you are at the helm.
Farewell green shores.
On board we have all which can gladden human
heart.
Love, danger,
Music and wine.

Hoist the sail, let us away.
Oh my boat,
At some time, all is over. Towards the brink of the
depths
Your path is after all
Destined to run.

Then, oh sea, take me, and let
The beating of our hearts sound together day and
night.
Let your streams run through my eyes
Like a string of beautiful green dreams.
Far down in the depths of your embrace, my ear
will,
Like the conch, keep faith and always hear.

The old song!

I am the unbounded sea.
No other gods shalt thou have.
For all eternity I remain unchanging.
My pleasure is more than earthly pleasure.
And my sorrow is more than earthly sorrow.
One and undivided am I.
Come, oh free hearts, to mine.

Hoist the sail, weigh anchor.
Everything of substance vanishes.
The moon comes,
Shines in everything,
Farewell river and harbour,
Your gulls still follow the ship.
How the waves of the open sea
Run against our bow.

Echo left we behind,
Miles of distance and the moon also.
Let your soul, your blood
Echo mine.
Oh shore, farewell,
Eternal are the sea's delights,
Eternal, oh eternal
Delights.
(Exeunt)
      (Curtain)

Select Bibliography

The most comprehensive bibliography of Isak Dinesen's work and critical studies of it can be found in Robert Langbaum's *The Gayety of Vision*, pp. 287–292. In the following I have restricted myself to material used directly in writing this study. Wherever details of first editions are given together with an edition in brackets, the latter has been used in this book and is the source of any quotations.

All references to miscellaneous papers and manuscripts are to those formerly kept at Rungstedlund, but now in the Royal Library, Copenhagen. The Royal Library has made a detailed catalogue, but as a brief indication of the contents of these papers, they include: some early short plays, some poems, drafts of stories in Danish and English, either complete or fragmentary, diaries from 1906 and 1910, some notes for various lectures, working drafts of various articles, early sketch-books, some school exercise-books, albums of photographs from Kenya and records of safari, lists of proposed subjects, working notes for stories.

I *BOOKS BY ISAK DINESEN*

In English:

Isak Dinesen: *Seven Gothic Tales*, Harrison Smith & Robert Haas, New York, 1934; Putnam, London, 1934.
(Modern Library, New York, 1934.)

Karen Blixen: *Out of Africa*, Putnam, London, 1937; as Isak Dinesen: Random House, New York, 1952.
(Modern Library, New York, 1952.)

Isak Dinesen: *Winter's Tales*, Putnam, London, 1942; Random House, New York, 1942.
(Vintage Books, New York, 1942.)

Pierre Andrézel: *The Angelic Avengers*, Putnam, London, 1946; Random House, New York, 1947.
(Putnam, London, 1946.)

Isak Dinesen: *Last Tales*, Putnam, London, 1957; Random House, New York, 1957.
(Random House, New York, 1957.)

Isak Dinesen: *Anecdotes of Destiny*, Michael Joseph, London, 1958; Random House, New York, 1958.
(Random House, New York, 1958.)

Isak Dinesen: *Shadows on the Grass*, Michael Joseph, London, 1960; Random House, New York, 1960.
(Random House, New York, 1960.)

Isak Dinesen: *Ehrengard*, Michael Joseph, London, 1963; Random House, New York, 1963.
(Random House, New York, 1963.)

Karen Blixen: *The Revenge of Truth*, © 1960 Gyldendalske Boghandel, Nordisk Forlag A/S. A non-exclusive licence to include *The Revenge of Truth, A Marionette Comedy*, by Karen Blixen has been granted to Putnam & Co. Ltd. by the owners of the copyright, The Rungstedlund Foundation, Rungstedlund, Denmark.

In Danish :

Isak Dinesen: *Syv fantastiske Fortællinger*, Reitzel, Copenhagen, 1935.
(Gyldendal, Copenhagen, 1950.)

Karen Blixen: *Den afrikanske Farm*, Gyldendal, Copenhagen, 1937.
(Gyldendal, Copenhagen, 1942.)

Karen Blixen: *Vinter-Eventyr*, Gyldendal, Copenhagen, 1942.

Pierre Andrézel: *Gengældelsens Veje*, translated into Danish by Clara Svendsen sic, Gyldendal, Copenhagen, 1944.

Karen Blixen: *Sidste Fortællinger*, Gyldendal, Copenhagen, 1957.

Karen Blixen: *Skæbne-Anekdoter*, Gyldendal, Copenhagen, 1958.

Karen Blixen: *Skygger på Græsset*, Gyldendal, Copenhagen, 1960.

Osceola, edited by Clara Svendsen, Gyldendal, Copenhagen, 1962. Contains the following short stories in Danish together

with seven early poems also in Danish. Dates of first publication are given in brackets:
'Grjotgard Ålvesøn og Aud' (previously unpublished).
'Pløjeren' (1907).
'Eneboerne' (1907).
'Familien de Cats' (1909).
Poems: 'Vinger'; 'Maaneskin'; 'Medvind'; 'Vuggesang'; 'En Stjerne'; 'Balladen om mit Liv'; 'Ex Africa'.
Karen Blixen: *Ehrengard*, translated into Danish by Clara Svendsen, Gyldendal, Copenhagen, 1963.

II *ESSAYS, ARTICLES & MINOR WORKS BY ISAK DINESEN*

K.B.–F. 'Sandhedens Hævn: En Marionetkomedie', *Tilskueren*, May, 1926, pp. 329–344. (As Karen Blixen: Gyldendal, Copenhagen, 1960.)

Isak Dinesen: 'Karyatiderne: En ufuldendt fantastisk Fortælling', *Bonniers Litterära Magasin*, March, 1938, pp. 166–193.

Karen Blixen: 'Hartvig Frisch som Nabo' in *Hartvig Frisch*, pp. 26–32; Fremad, Copenhagen, 1950.

Isak Dinesen: 'The Ghost Horses', *Ladies' Home Journal*, October, 1951, pp. 56 ff. (*Spøgelseshestene*, Fremad, Copenhagen, 1966).

Isak Dinesen: 'On Mottoes of My Life', New York, 1960. (As Karen Blixen: Presentation Books, Danish Ministry of Foreign Affairs, Copenhagen, 1962.)

Karen Blixen: Introduction to Basil Davidson, *Det genfundne Afrika*, Gyldendal, Copenhagen, 1962.

Karen Blixen: Introduction to Truman Capote, *Holly*, Gyldendal, Copenhagen, 1960.

Karen Blixen: 'Rungstedlund: En radio-tale' in *Hilsen til Otto Gelsted*, pp. 18–41; Sirius, Århus, 1958.

Karen Blixen: *Essays*, Gyldendal, Copenhagen, 1965. Contains the following essays with dates of first publication:
'Mit Livs Mottoer', (translated from English by Clara Svendsen), New York, 1960.

'Daguerreotypier', Copenhagen, 1951.
'En Baaltale med 14 Aars forsinkelse', Copenhagen, 1953.
'Fra Lægmand til Lægmand', Copenhagen, 1954.
'Breve fra et Land i Krig', Copenhagen, 1948.
'Gensyn med England', Copenhagen, 1948.
'Om Retskrivning', Copenhagen, 1938.
'H. C. Branner: *Rytteren*', Copenhagen, 1952.
'Karen Blixen fortæller', Lousiana Grammofonplader.

III STUDIES & SELECTED ARTICLES ON ISAK DINESEN & HER WORK

Brandt, Jørgen Gustava: 'Et Essay om Karen Blixen' in *Heretica*, Vol. VI, No. 2, pp. 200–223; No. 3, pp. 300–320, 1953.

Brix, Hans: *Karen Blixens Eventyr*, Gyldendal, Copenhagen, 1949.
Analyser og Problemer, Vol. VI, pp. 286–306, Gyldendal, Copenhagen, 1950.

Brostrøm, Torben: 'Karen Blixen' in *Dansk Litteratur Historie*, Vol. 4, pp. 195–210; Politikens Forlag, Copenhagen, 1966.

Cate, Curtis: 'Isak Dinesen', *Atlantic Monthly*, December, 1959, pp. 151–155.

Claudi, Jørgen: *Contemporary Danish Authors with a Brief Outline of Danish Literature*, pp. 109–114; Det Danske Selskab, Copenhagen, 1952.

Davenport, John: 'A Noble Pride. The Art of Karen Blixen', *The Twentieth Century*, March, 1956, pp. 264–274.

Elling, Christian: '*Karen Blixen*' in *Danske Digtere i det 20. Aarhundrede*, pp. 521–555; Gads Forlag, Copenhagen, 1951.

Frandsen, Ernst: 'Udsigt over et halvt Aarhundrede' in *Danske Digtere i det 20. Aarhundrede*, pp. 5–32, Gads Forlag, Copenhagen, 1951.

Gandrup, Richardt: *For og Imod. Kritik og Betragtning*, pp. 79–94; Gyldendal, Copenhagen, 1960.

Grandjean, Louis E.: *Blixens Animus, Et åndsorienteret forsøg*, Grandjeans Publications Fond, Copenhagen, 1957.

Hannah, Donald: 'In Memoriam Karen Blixen' in *The Sewanee Review*, Vol. LXXI, No. 4, pp. 585–604; Tennessee, 1963.

Henriksen, Aage: *Karen Blixen og Marionetterne*, Wivel, Copenhagen, 1952. (Later included in *Det guddommelige Barn og andre Essays om Karen Blixen*.)

Guder og galgefugle, Det Norske Studentersamfunds Kulturutvalg, Oslo, 1956.

Det guddommelige Barn og andre Essays om Karen Blixen Gyldendal, Copenhagen, 1965.

Johannesson, Eric O.: *The World of Isak Dinesen*, University of Washington Press, Seattle, 1961.

Kabell, Aage: *Karen Blixen debuterer*, Wilhelm Fink Verlag, Munich, 1968.

Kristensen, Tom: 'Syv fantastiske Fortællinger' in *Mellem Krigene. Artikler og Kroniker*, pp. 134–140. Gyldendal, Copenhagen, 1946.

Langbaum, Robert: *The Gayety of Vision. A Study of Isak Dinesen's Art*, Random House, New York, 1964.

Migel, Parmenia: *Titania. The Biography of Isak Dinesen*, Random House, New York, 1967.

Nielsen, Harald: *Karen Blixen. Studie i litterær Mystik*, Borgens Forlag, Copenhagen, 1956.

Petersen, Viggo Kjær: 'Karen Blixen' in *Danske Digtere i det 20. Aarhundrede* (revised edition), pp. 699–734; Gads Forlag, Copenhagen, 1966.

Poulsen, Kuno: 'Karen Blixens gamle og nye testamente' in *Vindrosen*, Vol. 10, No. 5, pp. 364–380; 1963.

Riisager, Vagn: *Karen Blixen*, Gyldendal, Copenhagen, 1952.

Rosendahl, Johannes: *Karen Blixen. Fire Foredrag*, Gyldendal, Copenhagen, 1957.

Svendsen, Clara & Lasson, Frans: *The Life and Destiny of Karen Blixen*, Random House, New York, 1970.

Svendsen, Clara & Wivel, Ole (editors): *Karen Blixen* [memorial anthology], Gyldendal, Copenhagen, 1962.

Svendsen, Clara: 'Karen Blixen som maler' in *Almanak*, Vol. I, No. 6, pp. 2–9; Århus, 1967.

Vogt, Per: 'Tilfellet Karen Blixen' in *Tendenser mot Tiden. Kulturessays og Portretter*, pp. 123–139; Tanum, Oslo, 1946.

Walter, Eugene: 'Isak Dinesen', *Paris Review*, No. 14, Autumn, 1956. pp. 43–59.
'Isak Dinesen conquers Rome', *Harper's Magazine*, February, 1965, pp. 46–54.
Wescott, Glenway: 'Isak Dinesen, the Storyteller', *Images of Truth. Remembrances and Criticism*, pp. 149–163, Hamish Hamilton, London, 1963.
With, Mette Klenow: 'Om Karen Blixen og hendes forfatterskab', *Karen Blixen. Et Udvalg*, pp. 178–221, Gyldendal, Copenhagen, 1964.

IV *NEWSPAPER INTERVIEWS*

Politiken, 1st May, 1934.
Berlingske Aftenavis, 24th June, 1950.
Politiken, 10th October, 1958.
Berlingske Tidende, 10th October, 1958.

V *GENERAL*

Blixen-Finecke, Bror: *African Hunter*, Cassell, London, 1937.
Boganis: *Jagtbreve og Nye Jagtbreve*, Gyldendal, Copenhagen, 1955.
Brandes, Georg: *Samlede Skrifter*, Vol. III, Gyldendal, Copenhagen, 1919.
Branner, H. C.: *Rytteren*, Branner og Korch's Forlag, Copenhagen, 1949. English translation: *The Riding Master*, London, 1951.
Daiches, David: *Literary Essays*, University of Chicago Press, Chicago, 1968.
Dinesen, Thomas: *No Man's Land*, Reitzel, Copenhagen, 1928. English translation: *Merry Hell! A Dane with the Canadians*, London, 1930.
Syrenbusken, Jesperson og Pios Forlag, Copenhagen, 1951. English translation: *Twilight on the Betzy*, London, 1952.
Duchartre, Pierre Louis: *The Italian Comedy*, Dover Publications Inc., New York, 1966.
Edel, Leon (ed.): *Henry James. The Future of the Novel*, Vintage Books, New York, 1956.

Eglinton, John: [W. K. Magee]: *A Memoir of AE: George William Russell*, Macmillan, London, 1937.

Ellmann, Richard: *Yeats: The Man and the Masks*, Dutton, New York, 1961.

Huxley, Elspeth: *White Man's Country. Lord Delamere and the Making of Kenya*, 2 vols. new edition: Chatto & Windus, London, 1953.

Settlers of Kenya, Longmans, London, 1948.

Kenya Today, Lutterworth Press, London, 1954.

The Flame Trees of Thika. Memories of an African Childhood, Penguin Books, London, 1962.

The Mottled Lizard, Chatto & Windus, London, 1962.

Forks and Hope. An African Notebook, Chatto & Windus, London, 1964.

Kleist, Heinrich von: 'Über das Marionettentheater', *Sämtliche Werke*, pp. 882–888, Droemer, Munich, 1952.

Murry, J. Middleton: *Keats*, fourth revised edition, Noonday Press, New York, 1955.

Nicoll, Allardyce: *The World of Harlequin*, C.U.P., London, 1963.

Ohrt, F.: *Udvalgte Sønderjydske Folkesagn*, Schønberg, Copenhagen, 1919.

Ortega y Gasset, José: *The Dehumanization of Art and Other Writings on Art and Culture*, Doubleday Anchor Books, New York, 1956.

Pirandello, Luigi: *Six Characters in Search of an Author* (translated by Frederick May), Heinemann, London, 1960.

Santayana, George: *Soliloquies in England and Later Soliloquies*, C. Scribner's Sons, New York, 1923.

Wellek, René: *A History of Modern Criticism*, Vol. II, Yale University Press, New Haven, 1955.

Yeats, W. B.: *Autobiographies*, Macmillan, London, 1955.

Mythologies, Macmillan, London, 1959.

A Vision, Macmillan, New York, 1961.

Wilde, Oscar: *Poems and Essays*, Collins, London, 1956.

INDEX

Index